THE

EPISTLE TO THE GALATIANS,

IN

GREEK AND ENGLISH,

WITH AN ANALYSIS AND EXEGETICAL COMMENTARY.

BY

SAMUEL H. TURNER, D. D.,

PROFESSOR OF BIBLICAL LITERATURE AND INTERPRETATION OF SCRIPTURE IN THE THEOLOGICAL
SEMINARY OF THE PROTESTANT EPISCOPAL CHURCH, AND OF THE HEBREW LANGUAGE
AND LITERATURE IN COLUMBIA COLLEGE, NEW YORK, AND
AUTHOR OF COMMENTARIES ON THE HEBREWS,
ROMANS AND EPHESIANS.

WIPF & STOCK · Eugene, Oregon

Wipf and Stock Publishers
199 W 8th Ave, Suite 3
Eugene, OR 97401

The Epistle to the Galatians in Greek and English
With an Analysis and Exegetical Commentary
By Turner, Samuel H
ISBN 13: 978-1-62564-882-2
Publication date 4/17/2014
Previously published by Dana and Co., 1856

CONTENTS.

PREFACE.

———◦◖◗◦———

It was my original intention to publish this Commentary on the Epistle to the Galatians in connection with that on the Ephesians. But, at the very time when the manuscript was about to be sent to the press, I saw an announcement of Jowett's work on this Epistle,[*] and therefore determined to defer the publication of my own, until I should have had an opportunity of examining the production of this Oxford scholar. Whether the delay has been productive of any particular gain to the exposition now presented to the church must be left to the judgment of the orthodox, intelligent, and competent reader.

I will not hesitate to say, however, that Mr. Jowett's exposition has not given me satisfaction. In many respects it is quite meagre, and in some exceedingly vague and indefinite, not to say, of doubtful orthodoxy. He does not always fully and clearly develop his meaning; and the obscurity which marks his expositions not unfrequently affects portions which, as they relate to Christian doctrines, ought to be placed in a clear light. I have not taken any very particular notice of his remarks on such portions, simply because to discuss properly the subject of them would have compelled me to object to or modify many of his positions, and to go more largely into detail than would comport with my purpose. Several statements, too, in his Introduction, might well be controverted, and shown to bear unfavorably on that prominent character and authority which may rightfully be claimed for this Epistle of St. Paul. The work of the Oxford Fellow and Tutor cannot be allowed to add very much to our store of Biblical Interpretation.

The delay just spoken of has happily made me acquainted with another late English production on this Epistle, by the Rev. Mr.

* The Epistle of St. Paul to the Galatians, with critical notes and dissertations. By Benjamin Jowett, M. A., Fellow and Tutor of Balliol College, Oxford. London, 1855,

Ellicott.* This book, as a critical and grammatical Commentary, is worthy of the highest commendation. No doubt it will be duly appreciated by carefully trained English scholars. It is earnestly hoped that our own theological students and younger clergy will become acquainted with a work, which lays in true grammatical principles the solid foundation of safe interpretation. The careful investigation which distinguishes this volume is only equalled by the truly Christian spirit which evidently governs the author. His ruling principles seem to be, love of truth, profound regard for the inspired character of the New Testament, and right appreciation of the divine system of the Gospel. An examination of this Commentary has served to confirm the opinion, that the sound interpreter must also be the sound grammarian; and I will not hesitate to acknowledge, that it compels me to lament the want of that training which alone can produce in the requisite degree such qualification. May the rising generation of Biblical students feel and act upon the principles which Mr. Ellicott has stated in the former part of his preface; and may all our Academies and Colleges, which have in view the extension of Christian truth and an acquaintance with the revealed documents which embody it, carefully, accurately, and thoroughly instruct their classes in that knowledge of Greek, which is the only solid human groundwork of New Testament interpretation. I cannot but add my expression of regret, that the author seems to have limited himself too much to grammatical investigations, so that his interpretations are sometimes less full than might be desired.

The reader must not be surprised or disappointed if, in the following work, he should find that, on some few points, I have not ventured to express a decided opinion in favor of one among several interpretations of particular passages. I hold it to be a great and important principle in the exposition of Scripture, as it is also in the illustration of the divine volume of nature, to advance in opinion just so far as the accessible and clearly settled data allow; and, consequently, when these are not sufficiently full or clear to justify an explicit, unequivocal, and decided expression of the meaning, thus to confess a proper degree of ignorance and uncertainty. In the inquiring, thoughtful, and judicious mind, unfounded assertion can never be made the substitute of satisfactory

---

* A Critical and Grammatical Commentary on St. Paul's Epistle to the Galatians, with a revised Translation. By C. J. Ellicott, M. A., Rector of Pilton, Rutland, and late Fellow of St. John's College, Cambridge. London, 1854.

proof. It is better to acknowledge uncertainty than to decide with an air of positive and dogmatic infallibility. For this reason, I could not venture to express a decided opinion on some very difficult passages. Such decisions must be left for future investigators of Biblical truth. God grant that the number of such may abound; that, while "many shall run to and fro," divine knowledge may be increased; that, as demonstrative science is gradually developing the truths of God contained in the great book of nature, so careful and profound investigation of his written word may make clear the divine counsels comprehended within the equally at least great book of revelation. When both shall have been investigated critically, painfully, thoroughly, religiously, with the faith which makes the intellect, feeling its humanity and consequently its imperfection, yield to the superiority of clearly ascertained divine decisions, as affirmed in the Hebrew and Greek Scriptures; then truly shall we begin to "see eye to eye." Then indeed shall we be able to proclaim to the world, that we are what we profess to be, CHRISTIANS, who regard the Sacred Scriptures as the sole ultimate rule of faith. Then shall *the teachers* of this truly Evangelical, divine system, embodied in the written word, when called on for "a reason of the hope that is in" them, appeal to the Hebrew and Greek Bible, and say, THUS AND THUS IT IS WRITTEN.

GENERAL THEOLOGICAL SEMINARY.
July, 1856.

INTRODUCTION.

ABOUT the year 280 before Christ,[*] numerous parties of Gauls emigrated from their native land, and sought a more southern residence. Under the guidance of two of their leaders, Leonarius and Lotharius, multitudes passed beyond the Bosphorus, and at last settled in Asia Minor. Becoming incorporated with the Greeks that inhabited this region of country, they acquired in some degree their language, and became known as Gallo-Græcians, or, by contraction, Galatians. It was to the descendants of these settlers that St. Paul addressed this Epistle.

The Galatians had been converted to Christianity by this Apostle. Jowett, indeed, does not hesitate to say that " it is not possible to give a perfectly certain and definite answer to the question, whether the Church was founded by the Apostle himself."[†] But St. Paul plainly alludes to his own laborious efforts to make them acquainted with the Gospel, when he employs the very impressive figurative language, " My dear children, of whom *I travail in birth again*, until Christ be formed in you :" iv. 19. During which of his journeys their conversion took place is somewhat uncertain. In Acts xv. 36, he proposes to Barnabas to make a visit to those Christians to whom they had before preached the Gospel. In consequence of a private difference of opinion, in which neither of these good men thought proper to yield, Paul made his excursion in company with Silas: ver. 40. In xvi. 6, we find them travelling " throughout the region of Galatia." The Asia in which the latter clause of the verse tells us they were forbidden to preach the word, is to be understood in the limited sense of Proconsular Asia, that is, the Western Provinces of Asia Minor, and consequently does not include Galatia, where no doubt they proclaimed the good tidings of salvation. Unless the

---

[*] See Prideaux' Connection of the Old and New Testaments, under the years 279–277 before Christ, and the writers there referred to.

[†] Introduction, p. 186.

Apostle comprehended within his circuit districts of country not before visited, the Galatians must have been previously converted to the faith. If so, this event may have taken place at the period mentioned in xiv. 6, when Paul and Barnabas, to avoid an attempted persecution, "fled unto Lystra and Derbe, cities of Lycaonia, and unto the region that lieth round about, and preached the Gospel there." As Galatia lay some distance north of this vicinity, it has been inferred that, on this occasion, Christianity was first made known to its inhabitants. But, in opposition to this theory, it is with reason maintained, that the language in xiv. 6 "cannot be extended to Galatia without comprehending a wide range of country," and must therefore be confined to the immediate vicinity of the cities there mentioned, which lay on "the other side of Lycaonia away from Galatia, and not on the side of Lycaonia next it. When Paul was driven from Iconium, he came to Lystra and Derbe, that is, towards the south. But Galatia was situated to the north, being separated from Lycaonia by Phrygia intervening." And, although it was St. Paul's chief purpose to visit during this tour those churches which he had been formerly instrumental in founding, yet there is no reason to suppose, that he limited his efforts in behalf of the Gospel exclusively to their confirmation in the faith. The conversion of the Galatians, therefore, may have taken place, at this time. An hypothesis has been lately advanced by some German writers, that the Christians of Lycaonia, and chiefly those of Lystra and Derbe, are meant by the Galatians whom St. Paul converted to the Gospel, and to whom he addressed his Epistle. But it has been proved to be wholly unfounded, and is almost universally rejected by the critics. This theory and the subject immediately before noted, are both discussed by Davidson* and Olshausen,† to whom the reader is referred for fuller information.—On a subsequent occasion we find St. Paul visiting the Galatians again and strengthening their faith: xviii. 23.

The time and place of writing the Epistle have been very much disputed. The various opinions which different commentators and critics have defended are given in detail by Davidson.‡ Some, both ancient and modern, follow the subscription appended to it. This presumes the letter to have been written, not earlier than A. D. 61, during St. Paul's imprisonment at Rome, though without determin-

* Introduction to the New Testament, London, 1849, vol. ii., pp. 288 et seq.
† Commentary on Galatians, Introduction, (English translation,) Edinburgh, 1851, pp. 2 et seq.
‡ Ubi sup., p. 292.

ing whether at an early or late period of his confinement there. But it is well known by Biblical scholars that the subscriptions are of much later date than the Epistles themselves, and were added not earlier than the 4th or 5th century, and probably by Euthalius of the latter. Their accuracy is not to be relied on. Nothing therefore can be inferred from any argument drawn from this source.

On the other hand, some have regarded it as the first of St. Paul's epistles, written about the year 51. This assumes the earliest date before mentioned of the conversion of the Galatians, that namely which assigns it to the time referred to in Acts xiv. 6. But if this were even conceded, it would not follow that the letter was written so very soon after their conversion; as the text which may be thought to sustain it, (Gal. i. 6,) may well be supposed to allude to their original establishment in the faith as narrated in Acts xvi. 6.

If, as the best critics seem to admit, the account in this latter passage of the Acts does refer to the original visit of St. Paul to the Galatians, and consequently to their conversion, then it will follow, taking into consideration statements and allusions contained in the Epistle itself, that it must have been composed not long after his second visit mentioned in Acts xviii. 23. In defence of this view Gal. iv. 13 has often been appealed to. "At the first" has been thought to imply two occasions at least of preaching the Gospel to them. But, although the view is in itself probable, the phrase is quite too indefinite to settle such a point, as it might certainly be employed, if the Apostle had been at Galatia but once. Still, the character, degree and extent of the error which so thoroughly pervaded the Galatian church, and the strong prejudices which many in that community had imbibed against the Apostle, must have required some time to grow to such a height; and their former laudable Christian character and conduct, and the respect and affection with which they once regarded their spiritual father, could hardly have become so completely changed, without the natural influence of time and gradually operating circumstances: See iii. 4, iv. 15, v. 7. The language of i. 6, " I marvel that ye are so soon removed unto another Gospel," only shows that their change from truth to error was comparatively rapid, and the expression " so soon" may as well be supposed to allude to the second visit of Acts xviii. 23, as to that of their conversion implied in xvi. 6.

If, then, as is most probable, the Epistle were written not long after the second visit, its date may be assigned to the year 55, and

Ephesus, to which city the Apostle soon afterwards went, (xix. 1,) may be regarded as the place of its composition. Certain objections, which have been advanced against this view, are stated and refuted by Davidson.* They are chiefly of a negative character, and not sufficiently important to make any particular notice of them necessary in this brief Introduction.

The Galatian church consisted of Jewish and Gentile converts, and the false teachers under whose influence they had unhappily been brought, maintained that the Mosaic ritual was equally obligatory on both parties for their justification and acceptance with God. In opposition to this erroneous system, St. Paul affirms that Christ hath set all true Christians free from this yoke of bondage. The supposition that there was only one leading teacher of this and similar errors, cannot be sustained. The ritualistic party was numerous, and no doubt had several defenders zealous of their heretical views. The occasional use of the singular number in speaking of them is not at all inconsistent with this opinion. Of what particular class among the Galatian Christians the party opposed to St. Paul consisted, it is not easy to determine. Some suppose them to have been Gentile converts, who had been led to connect Judaism with Christianity. Others consider them as having been originally proselytes to Judaism, who subsequently embraced the Gospel. And others again regard them as native Jews, who, becoming converts to the Christian faith, were the more easily induced, by old associations and habits, to return to the observance of the ritual law. It is neither necessary nor practicable to determine positively which of these views is the most correct; indeed it may well be doubted whether the opposing party consisted of any one of the three classes exclusively. In all probability the larger proportion of them was of the first or third.

These persons seem to have attacked St. Paul's apostolic and independent authority, and also the consistency of his character and conduct. Both these points he vindicates at length, especially in the first and second chapters. "He demonstrates his own apostolic dignity, as resting on a direct call and revelation from Christ, and as acknowledged by the older Apostles themselves."* His opponents taught also a fundamentally erroneous view of justification, requiring, in addition to faith in Christ, obedience to the Mosaic law, especially the ceremonial part of it. This most mischievous error the Apostle effectually refutes. "He draws out a masterly de-

* Ubi sup., p. 298 et seq.
† Schaff's History of the Apostolic Church, New York, 1853, § 77, p. 283.

velopment of the Gospel as distinguished from the Law, and of the living faith which alone makes us children of God and heirs of the promise."* He shows the absurdity of founding any hope of salvation on merely outward observances, or such imperfect moral obedience as fallen man can render, and proves that it can be obtained only by a living faith in the Lord Jesus Christ. In this respect the Epistle coincides with one of the leading topics discussed in that to the Romans.

Dr. Davidson† has given a list of parallel places in these two Epistles, which, with the exception of the three last, are here introduced.

Galatians ii. 16	Romans iii. 20.
19	vii. 4
iii. 6	iv. 2.
7	12; ix. 6, 7.
13	viii. 1–4.
iv. 4	3.
5, 6	14–17.
28	ix. 7.
v. 14	xiii. 8–10.
17	vii. 13–24.
19–21	i. 28–31.
vi. 1, 2	xv. 1–3.

Among the works consulted or referred to in the following commentary, it may be proper to mention particularly that of ELIAS ANNES BORGER, as especially worthy of attention. It is an able exposition of the Galatians, containing learned Prolegomena, critical notes to determine the correct text, and a full and carefully prepared exegetical commentary on the whole Epistle. The book is an Inaugural Hermeneutical Specimen, submitted on occasion of the author's being admitted to the degree of D. D. in the royal university of Holland. It was published at Leyden in 1807 in one 8vo volume of 399 pages. It is a learned, judicious and valuable work.

* Schaff, ubi sup. † Ubi sup. p. 326.

ANALYSIS

OF THE

EPISTLE TO THE GALATIANS.

———————

SECTION I.

Chap. I–II.

THE AUTHOR CLAIMS AN IMMEDIATE DIVINE APPOINTMENT TO THE APOS-
TOLIC OFFICE. HE GIVES A SKETCH OF PART OF HIS EARLIER LIFE.
MENTIONS HIS RECOGNITION AS AN APOSTLE BY HIS ELDER BRETH-
REN. HIS CENSURE OF ST. PETER. SHOWS HIS CONSISTENCY IN WITH-
STANDING THE ATTEMPT TO IMPOSE THE JEWISH RITUAL ON GENTILE
CONVERTS.

St. Paul begins by declaring that his Apostolic character and authority
did not spring from any human source, or come to him through any
human channel, but by commission directly from Christ and God. In
writing to the Christian communities of Galatia, he unites along with
himself the brethren who were with him, and invokes a blessing from God
and from Christ, who gave himself for our redemption in accordance with
the will of his father, to whom the Apostle offers an ascription of praise:
i. 1–5.

He expresses his surprise that the Galatians are so soon turning away
from God, who had favored them with the blessings of the Gospel, to a
false system, which is not to be regarded as another Gospel. He recollects,
however, that they have been subjected to the mischievous efforts of certain troublesome persons, who were desirous of subverting the Gospel.
He expresses his abhorrence of any attempt to set up a system contrary
to that which he had proclaimed. He employs the strongest possible
language, which he repeats in order to make his declaration the more
emphatic, imprecating destruction on whatever being should rashly make
the effort: 6–9.

The Apostle's opponents appear to have charged him with versatility,

1

with inconsistency of conduct, and a censurable accommodation to the views and practices of different religious parties, perverting probably the meaning of his own avowal : "I was made all things to all men, that I might by all means save some:" 1 Cor. ix. 22. He therefore proceeds to vindicate himself from such a charge.—Is it the favor of man or of God that I endeavor to conciliate ? Is my object to please men ? If it were, I should be unworthy of the name of Christ's servant. I tell you that the Gospel as proclaimed by me, was not in accordance with nor adapted to human weakness; for I was not instructed in it from any human source, but by revelation from Christ himself. You have heard of my former course of life when a Jew, how severely I persecuted the church, and endeavored to destroy it. And I advanced in a knowledge of the Jewish system of religion beyond many of the same age with myself, being extraordinarily zealous for traditional law and usage. But when, at my conversion, God, who from my very birth determined to call me by his gracious intervention, was pleased to make known to me the Gospel of his Son, that I might proclaim the glad tidings thereof among the Gentiles; immediately, without conferring with men or going to Jerusalem for sanction from those who were Apostles before me, I went away to Arabia, and afterwards returned to Damascus: 10–17. It was not until three years after my conversion and call to the Apostolic office, that I went to Jerusalem to visit Peter, with whom I remained only fifteen days, without seeing any other Apostle, except James, the Lord's brother. I aver in the presence of God, that all the foregoing statements are true. Afterwards, I went to Syria and Cilicia, still being personally unknown to the Christian churches of Judea. Only they had heard that the former persecutor had become a preacher of the Gospel, for which they glorified God : 18–24.

The author then proceeds to say that fourteen years afterwards, dating either from his conversion or from his leaving Jerusalem, he returned to the capital in company with Barnabas and Titus; that he went there in consequence of a divine revelation, and explained the tenor and character of the Gospel as announced by him to the Gentiles, but only in a private way to some of the more distinguished Christian teachers; that he did this to remove all occasion of censure or misapprehension, lest his efforts in behalf of Christianity should be made ineffectual; and that Titus, although a Greek, was not obliged to be circumcised: ii. 1–3. But, he goes on to state, I made this journey and explanation on account of false brethren clandestinely introduced to act as spies on our Christian liberty, in order to enslave us to the ritual law; to whom myself and Barnabas and other defenders of the Gospel did not yield for a moment, in order to preserve the truth inviolate for you and other converts. But from those distinguished persons of whom I have spoken—however great their elevation, it does not affect me, for God regards no human distinction—I received neither instruction nor authority. On the contrary, when they perceived, from the conference which was held, and also from other sources of inform- ation, that I had been entrusted with proclaiming the Gospel to the Gentiles, as Peter had been with disseminating it among the Jews, the same divine being who had wrought in Peter for the one class having wrought also in me for the other; and when they knew the favor which had thus been bestowed on me, these distinguished persons, James, Peter and John, who were evidently pillars of the church, cordially received Barnabas and myself as coadjutors, we preaching to the Gentiles and they to the Jews. Only they were solicitous that we should remember and assist the poor Christians of Judea, as I also was desirous of doing: 4–10.

The Apostle now introduces the conduct of St. Peter when at Antioch, and his own censure passed upon him on account of his culpable course. Previously to the coming from St. James of certain Jewish converts still zealous for the law, he had not scrupled to hold familiar intercourse with the Gentiles; but afterwards, fearing the censure of the rigid Judaizers, he withdrew from them. Other Jewish converts and Barnabas himself, were led astray by this hypocritical behavior. When St. Paul saw that they did not conduct themselves with that steady regard to truth and propriety which the Gospel required, he confronted his elder Apostolic brother publicly, and charged him with inconsistency: 11–14. ' If thou, a Jew by birth and education, livest in general like a Gentile, free from the obligation of the Jewish ritual law, how is it that now thou wouldst compel the Gentile converts to submit to the restraints imposed by that law? We are Jews by nature and not Gentile sinners. But, knowing that a man is not justified by obedience to the law, but only by faith in Christ, even we have believed in Christ, in order to obtain justification by faith in him, and not by obedience to the law, for by such obedience no one can be justified. But if even we, after seeking thus to be justified through Christ, are nevertheless found to be unpardoned sinners, is Christ the min- ister of sin? Is the failure to be charged on him? This would be the unavoidable result, inasmuch as he hath established this method of justifi- cation, and commissioned us to proclaim it. But God forbid that we should give the least sanction to any such conclusion:' 14–17. The writer then turns to his Galatian converts. He defends his own consistency, declaring that were he to rear up as a means of justification the edifice of the ritual law which he had been pulling down, he should make himself a transgres- sor. But so far from doing this, he affirms that, in consequence of the in- efficiency of the law, he has become dead to it, he is unaffected by it, that through the Gospel he may live to God's glory. He then amplifies both the figure and its application, representing himself as crucified with Christ, meaning, to the world and all its tempting offers. No longer does he live by merely natural agencies; it is Christ who lives in him, as the guiding, influencing, and controlling principle of his being; his present life is carried on by faith in the Son of God who loved and redeemed him. He does not annul the grace of God by setting up any external observances as a ground of justification; for could justification be attained in such a way, then Christ's death had been useless: 18–21.

SECTION II.

Chap. III.

THE INCONSISTENCY AND FOLLY OF ABANDONING THE GOSPEL FOR THE LAW, IN ORDER TO OBTAIN JUSTIFICATION. THE COVENANT MADE BY GOD WITH ABRAHAM AND HIS SPIRITUAL PROGENY NOT ANNULLED BY THE SUBSEQUENT LAW OF MOSES. THIS WAS ONLY DISCIPLINARY AND PREPARATORY TO THE GOSPEL, WHICH EMBRACES WITHIN THE RANGE OF ITS BLESSINGS, AND UNITES MOST INTIMATELY TOGETHER, ALL CONDITIONS OF MEN.

THE author expresses his amazement at the strange folly of the Galatians, who had been so fully and particularly instructed in the true nature of the Gospel, in preferring an external carnal system to a spiritual one, thus forfeiting their claim to all its advantages. The gifts of the Spirit, the power of working miracles, spring from faith. He refers to the blessing promised to Abraham, and through him to the nations in general, and particularly to the faithful. But those who depend upon the law are subjected to the curse denounced against the disobedient. Justification is attainable only by faith. But this is a principle which the law does not recognize; it speaks only of doing its commands, and of living thereby. From the curse which it denounces Christ has delivered us, having himself submitted to its infliction, that, through faith in him, the Gentiles might become partakers of the spiritual promise made to the father of the faithful: 1–14.

The Apostle had commenced this chapter by addressing the Galatians as senseless or inconsiderate. He now changes the style of his appeal, accosting them kindly as brethren, and argues with them. He lays down the simple yet fundamental principle, that even human covenants, after they have been ratified, are neither to be annulled nor added to. He then states that the promises were made to Abraham and his progeny. He explains the meaning and application of the word used in the singular to denote this progeny, affirming that it does not comprehend all the various races and classes of the patriarch's descendants, but is limited to one class, the spiritual progeny, that is, Christ as the head of his mystical body of true believers; and thus comprehends as a necessary consequence, the believers themselves as being his members. He maintains that the covenant thus ratified by God with reference to Christ, the law, which was promulgated hundreds of years afterwards, did not annul, so as to make the promise void. For if this had been the case, and the blessing of a heavenly inheritance had come from the law, it would not have been the result of the promise. But this could not be, since God gave Abraham gracious assurance of it through promise. The inquiry, why then was the law given, is answered briefly, as it is more fully in 'Romans vii., on account of man's transgressions, and to prepare him for the Gospel; and it was intended to be of force until the great progeny, Christ, in whom the promise had its fulfilment, should come, having been gloriously established by means of angels through Moses, its mediator. This seems to suggest the remark, that the very idea of a mediator implies two parties; or else this, that, unlike Moses and every other, the great Mediator is not a mediator of one nation or body of men, but of all mankind, and that God is one and the same, the only God, and consequently, the God of all : 15–20.

The author resumes his train of remark. Are then the laws and the promises of God at variance with each other? Certainly not. If the law could have removed the effects of sin and given pardon and life to the sinner, justification would have been attainable by it. But it could not secure these blessings, on account, as he states in Rom. viii. 3, of human sinfulness. Therefore the Scripture represents all men as under the dominion of sin, that the promise of happiness through Christ, might be made and verified to believers. Until the Gospel came, we were kept confined and strictly guarded, as it were, under the control of the law. He now introduces this law, by a change of figure, as a harsh teacher of man while in a state of religious pupilage, thus preparing him for justification by faith. But when the Gospel has come, he is released from the supervision and discipline of such a preparatory teacher. For it is by faith in Christ that all become the sons of God, whosoever have been truly and fully baptized into Christ having become assimilated to and united with him. In this state of holy union, and as belonging thereto, all external distinctions, whether of former religious profession, or of civil condition, or of sex, are done away. The whole body of such are most intimately united to Christ. And being so, they are Abraham's spiritual progeny, and heirs in accordance with the original promise : 21–29.

SECTION III.

THE LEGAL AND CHRISTIAN CONDITIONS ILLUSTRATED. THE APOSTLE EX-
PRESSES HIS DEEP FEELING AT THE DEFECTION OF THE GALATIANS
FROM THEIR FORMER STATE OF CHRISTIAN CHARACTER.

THE author now proceeds to sketch briefly, but very graphically, a person's legal and Christian conditions in contrast with each other. He does this under the image of an heir, referring probably to the Roman usage of publicly recognizing a youth's arrival at the age of manhood, by investing him with the toga virilis. While in his minority, he is, as regards author-ity and independence, in the same condition as a slave, subject to the con-trol of his father, although in prospect he is lord of all the patrimonial inheritance. In this his state of inferiority, he is amenable to the officers appointed to superintend his education, and authorized to subject him, during this preparatory training, to proper subordination and discipline. This state of things continues until the time when the father shall deter-mine, in accordance either with law or usage, to bring it to a termination. Thus also is man in regard to his religious condition. While in his weak state of moral and spiritual childhood, he was conversant merely with the elements of religion, what may be called its rudiments. These are chiefly external, and therefore best adapted to a worldly and very imperfect spiritual state. But, on the arrival of the period when the divine plan was ready to be developed, God sent his Son, born into the world as a suffering human creature, and subject to the law, in order that, by his life of holy obedience and his adequate and satisfactory atonement, he might redeem those under the domination and sentence of the law from its ultimate curse, and thus make us his own children. And because we are thus made sons, God hath also sent the Holy Spirit, in the name and as the divine agent of his eternal Son, into our hearts, enabling us, with grateful effusions of joy, to regard him as our reconciled father. Hence it follows, O Christian, that thou art not a servant, as thou formerly wert before the Gospel came to thee in its quickening, energizing power, but a recognized son, and consequently an heir of God through Christ: 1–7.

The Apostle now directs his attention more particularly to the Gentile portion of the Galatian church. He tells them that, in their uncovenanted state, they had no right acquaintance with God, and paid slavish worship to

---

* Although this portion of the fourth chapter has a very intimate connection with the preceding one, I have thought it best, for the sake of convenience, to make it a separate section.

idols. But, on their conversion, they were brought to a proper knowledge of the true God; or rather, as with striking beauty he expresses it, (employing the word just used with the necessary change of its grammatical form,) they had been kindly regarded and favored by him. How then could they return to the trifling elementary principles, to which they were bent on again enslaving themselves, such as the very scrupulous, not to say superstitious observance of particular religious periods? He seems to regard all merely external ritualistic devotion, whether Jewish or Heathen, which did not conjoin with itself anything of the inward spirit of religion, as coming under the same category, and therefore speaks of their subjugation to the ritual law imposed by their false teachers, as if it were a relapse to Heathen ceremonies; and expresses his fear lest his labors among them had been useless. This strong manifestation of feeling and doubt, most probably prompts the immediately following language, which is perhaps to be regarded as an earnest entreaty to mutual affection. So far from considering them as having injured him by their course of conduct towards him, he reminds them that the physical weakness which impeded his first efforts in preaching the Gospel, was not regarded by them as a ground of contempt or degradation; that, on the contrary, they received him with the very highest respect and reverence; that so great was the felicity resulting from this affectionate union, that they would have done him any possible service, at the peril and loss of whatever was most precious: 8–15. But unhappily he has become their enemy by inculcating truth. The Apostle then warns them against the crafty efforts of their plausible false teachers. They show indeed a great zeal for you, but the motive is not good. Their desire is to exclude me from any share in your regard; or, (according to another and perhaps better reading,) to exclude you from any connection with me and God's church; and this, in order that all your zeal and affection may be concentrated on them. This suggests the remark, that it is laudable always to cherish and exercise zeal for what is good, and not merely during his presence with them. Then affectionately addressing them as his dear children, for whom he again labors in agony until the Christian character is rightly formed within them, he states his wish to be present among them, and to adapt his discourse and exhortation to their varying circumstances: 16–20.

SECTION IV.

THE INCONSISTENCY OF FALLING BACK UPON THE LAW FOR JUSTIFICATION
AND ACCEPTANCE WITH GOD, ILLUSTRATED BY AN ALLEGORICAL APPLI-
CATION OF A PART OF ABRAHAM'S HISTORY. CORRESPONDING EXHORTA-
TIONS AND WARNINGS.

ST. PAUL now points out to the Galatians the bearing which certain facts
in Abraham's life had on the error involved in their absurd preference of
the legal to the Christian system. The birth of Ishmael by the bond-
woman Hagar, according to the common course of nature, and of Isaac, by
Sarah the free woman, in an extraordinary manner and by virtue of a particular divine promise, are regarded as conveying an allegorical meaning.
The two women represent the Jewish and the Christian covenants. The
one proceeds from Mount Sinai, whose adherents are in a state of spiritual
servitude. This is symbolized by Hagar, (and the meaning of this very
word, which may express Mount Sinai in Arabia, agrees,) who corresponds
with Jerusalem in its present condition of bondage with her children.
Although he does not draw out the comparison between Sarah and the
Christian church in particular detail, he nevertheless comprehends it in the
remark, that the above Jerusalem, the Christian mother, is in a happy
state of freedom. Then, in the exulting words of Isaiah, he expresses her
joyous condition of reconciliation to her heavenly husband, and of being
blessed with innumerable spiritual offspring. True Christians, like Isaac, are
the children of the promise. As he who was born according to the course
of nature, ridiculed and showed a persecuting temper towards his brother,
whose birth was miraculous and under the influence of a special divine
promise and purpose; so now the carnally minded Jew, whose whole religion consists in external observances, persecutes the spiritually born
Christian. And as the son of the bond-woman was not allowed to share
the patriarchal inheritance with the more favored son of the free, and
therefore both he and his mother were expelled from the family; so Christians, being freeborn children of God, must steadfastly adhere to that
condition of glorious liberty in which Christ hath placed them, and not
suffer themselves to be confined by the oppressive yoke of legal bondage:
iv. 21, v. 1.

The Apostle then warns them that, if they depend upon circumcision
and the observance of the ritual law for justification, they have no benefit
to expect from Christ, inasmuch as they bind themselves to a full and perfect obedience. Whoever will seek to be justified by law sever thereby

their connection with him, and apostatize from his grace; for we can only expect justification through the Spirit by faith. Circumcision and uncircumcision are in themselves nothing; a living faith, showing its operation by love is everything. Ye did exert yourselves in the Christian course; who hindered your obedience to the truth? They who persuaded you to abandon it are opposing the will of God, who called you to the Gospel. The insidious influence, if not checked, will tend to pervade your whole body, and to mould your whole religious character. But I have a confidence with regard to you, that you will bend your minds to whatever is right and true; and those who trouble you must bear their own sentence. If, as I am calumniously accused by them, I maintain the necessity of circumcision and the Mosaic ritual, why am I subjected to persecution? Then truly has the cross ceased to be a stumbling block. O that those who endeavor to subvert your faith would cut themselves off! 2–12.

SECTION V.

CHAP. V. 13—VI. 10.

THE CHRISTIAN CONDITION ONE OF SPIRITUAL LIBERTY, AND REQUIRING CORRESPONDING LIFE AND CONDUCT. PRACTICAL DIRECTIONS.

THE Christian state of spiritual liberty gives no license to carnal indulgence, but requires the exercise of mutual love: 13–15. Under the guidance of the Spirit, fleshly lusts are controlled, and the spiritual element cherished. Then follow an enumeration of the principal developments of each: 16–25; also a deprecation of unchristian tempers; a direction how to treat a sinning brother; an exhortation to mutual assistance in difficulties; and a caution against inordinate self-esteem: 26, vi. 5. It is the duty of Christians to support their religious instructors. The character which any one cultivates, and the tenor of his habitual course of life, will produce corresponding results, whether of misery or happiness. While therefore opportunity is afforded we should habitually do good, and especially to those who are united to us by the close bonds of Christian fellowship: 6–10.

SECTION VI.

Chap. VI. 11–18.

CONCLUSION.

The Apostle, in order, doubtless to intimate his affection to the Galatians, and deep concern in their spiritual interests, appeals to the largeness of his letter, written entirely with his own hand, although, in ordinary cases, he employed an amanuensis. He then reverts again to the topic which occupied his thoughts, the efforts employed by the false teachers to induce them to be circumcised, which he ascribes to a desire to make a favorable impression, to avoid persecution, and to boast or exult in their success. But his only object of exultation was the cross of Christ. In the Christian condition nothing avails but a thorough internal change, and on them who lived in accordance therewith he invokes a blessing. He expresses his disregard of any future efforts that might be made to trouble him, as he bears on his person the marks of wounds inflicted on him for the cause, and proving him to be a servant, of Christ. In conclusion he invokes on the Galatians the blessing of Christ's grace: **11–18.**

COMMENTARY

EPISTLE TO THE GALATIANS.

SECTION I.

CHAP. I.—II.

THE AUTHOR CLAIMS AN IMMEDIATE DIVINE APPOINTMENT TO THE APOSTOLIC
OFFICE. HE GIVES A SKETCH OF PART OF HIS EARLIER LIFE—MENTIONS
HIS RECOGNITION AS AN APOSTLE BY HIS ELDER BRETHREN—HIS CENSURE
OF ST. PETER—SHOWS HIS CONSISTENCY IN WITHSTANDING THE ATTEMPT
TO IMPOSE THE JEWISH RITUAL ON GENTILE CONVERTS.

I. Παῦλος, ἀπόστολος οὐκ ἀπ'   PAUL, an apostle, not of men, I.
ἀνθρώπων οὐδὲ δι' ἀνθρώπου,   neither by man, but by Jesus
ἀλλὰ διὰ 'Ιησοῦ Χριστοῦ καὶ   Christ, and God the Father, who

---

CHAP. i. 1. As some of St. Paul's opponents appear to have questioned
his Apostolic authority, he is the more particular in the early part of the
Epistle to defend his claim to a direct divine commission, and this he does
by a very particular statement of facts. On this account it is best to give
to each of the prepositions here employed its distinct meaning, although
such is not their invariable usage. The former, ἀπό, expresses origin, and
the latter, διά, the medium of conveyance. This remark applies to the
first clause, but not to the second, where διά is used of Christ and God as
the source of his Apostolic authority, from and by whom it had been communicated. He denies that his Apostolic character and authority were derived from any human source, or conveyed to him through any human
channel; on the contrary, he affirms that he obtained them by means of
his divine call thereto by Christ himself.

Dr. Hammond regards the appointment related in Acts xiii. 2, 3, as the
ordination of Paul and Barnabas to be Apostles. He paraphrases thus:
"The Holy Spirit commanded them to ordain and consecrate Barnabas
and Saul to the Apostleship, to which God had already designed them."

2 raised him from the dead; and all   Θεοῦ πατρὸς τοῦ ἐγείραντος
   the brethren which are with me,   αὐτὸν ἐκ νεκρῶν, καὶ οἱ σὺν 2
   unto the churches of Galatia :   ἐμοὶ πάντες ἀδελφοί, ταῖς ἐκκλη-

---

On the text in Galatians, he allows both St. Paul's direct divine call to the
Gospel and his commission to "preach among the Gentiles;" but still
maintains that "after" these, "Acts xiii. 2, he was by special direction of
the Holy Ghost separated to the Apostleship." Archbishop Wake, in his
account of the epistle of Barnabas, Sect. 5, takes the same view of the
transaction recorded in the Acts. After mentioning Paul and Barnabas as
"discharging the work of a presbyter," he adds: "But they still wanted
the Apostolical or episcopal character. This dignity therefore we are told
they now received by the laying on of the hands of the other three prophets
there mentioned. St. Paul, though he were called to be an Apostle, not
by man, but by Jesus Christ himself, Gal. i., was yet consecrated to be an
Apostle by the ordinary form of imposition of hands." Olshausen also
takes the same general view of the verse before us and of the narrative in
the Acts.

But St. Paul's strong and definite and repeated assertions respecting
the divine origin and medium of his Apostleship are entirely at variance
with this theory, and so are the accounts of his call and allusions to it
contained in the Acts and elsewhere. See Acts ix. 5, 6, 15, 17, 20,
xx. 24, xxii. 14, 15, xxvi. 16, 19, 20, Gal. i. 1, 12, 16, ii. 6, 7, 9,
1 Tim. i. 12. The particular "work" for which Paul and Barnabas were
"separated" is related in Acts xiii. xiv., namely, to preach the Gospel
more extensively among the Gentiles; and, on their return to Antioch,
they are said to have accomplished it : xiv. 26.

Howson, in his account of this appointment of Barnabas and Saul,
states that "their final consecration and departure were the occasion of
another religious solemnity," after the divine command was given to "separate" them. But the narrative in the Acts contains no intimation of
more than one such "solemnity." It simply states that, as the prophets
and teachers were ministering to the Lord and fasting, the Holy Spirit
gave the direction, and that, having fasted and prayed, they obeyed the
divine injunction. There is not even an intimation of a second religious
service.

2. " The brethren" whom the Apostle connects with himself in this in-
scription may be those of his fellow laborers in the ministry who were his
companions at the time of writing. In his introductions to certain other
epistles, he associates with himself Timothy and Silvanus, and on one occasion Sosthenes, who may perhaps be comprehended within the same
class. See 1 Cor. i. 1, 2 Cor. i. 1, Phil. i. 1, Col. i. 1, 1 and 2 Thess. i. 1,
Philem. 1. But, on the other hand, as the phrase is general in meaning,

3 σίαις τῆς Γαλατίας· χάρις ὑμῖν καὶ εἰρήνη ἀπὸ θεοῦ πατρὸς καὶ κυρίου ἡμῶν Ἰησοῦ Χριστοῦ,
4 τοῦ δόντος ἑαυτὸν περὶ τῶν ἁμαρτιῶν ἡμῶν, ὅπως ἐξέληται ἡμᾶς ἐκ τοῦ ἐνεστῶτος αἰῶνος πονηροῦ κατὰ τὸ θέλημα τοῦ
5 θεοῦ καὶ πατρὸς ἡμῶν, ᾧ ἡ δόξα εἰς τοὺς αἰῶνας τῶν αἰώνων· ἀμήν.
6   Θαυμάζω, ὅτι οὕτω ταχέως

grace *be* to you, and peace, from 3 God the Father and *from* our Lord Jesus Christ, who gave himself for 4 our sins, that he might deliver us from this present evil world, according to the will of God and our Father; to whom *be* glory for ever 5 and ever : Amen.

I marvel that ye are so soon re- 6 moved from him that called you into the grace of Christ unto anoth-

---

" the brethren" intended may be his fellow Christians who were then with him. In either case, their concurrence in the letter confirms, by their joint attestation, the weight of the Apostle's representations.

4. " Who gave himself for our sins :" All scriptural language of this kind contains or implies the idea of atonement made for human sin by Christ's one sacrifice of himself. Comp. Matt. xx. 28, Mark x. 45, John vi. 51, 1 Tim. ii. 6, Tit. ii. 14, Heb. vii. 27, ix. 25–28, x. 10, 12, 14, 1 Pet. ii. 24. Jowett's note on this passage contains nothing but a tissue of assertions, which are neither proved nor capable of being proved. His conclusion " that, in general, the thing meant is that Christ took upon him human flesh, that he was put to death by sinful men, and raised men out of the state of sin, in this sense taking their sins upon himself," is a miserably meagre representation, Socinian in its bearing, and must be entirely unsatisfactory to a careful reader of Scripture.

" This present evil world," is equivalent to, ' our present condition of sinfulness and misery.'

6. The Apostle expresses his astonishment at the rapid declension of the Galatians from the truth of the Gospel. There is no sufficient reason for explaining *quickly* by *easily*, as Koppe does. The shortness of the time which had elapsed either since their conversion, or since the period of his late visit when he endeavored to establish them in the faith, is the prominent thought; the comparative facility with which their perversion had been effected is of course implied.

" Ye are removed," μετατίθεσθε· This rendering presumes the verb to be passive, and the removal to have already taken place. If it be middle, the apostasy will be represented as still going on, and the translation be, ' are removing, turning yourselves away.' To this effect are the expositions of Peile, Conybeare and Ellicott. Either of these views may be regarded as in harmony with the general contents of the Epistle, in some parts of which the author addresses the Galatians as having actually abandoned the truth, while in others he seems to represent them as in a trans-

7 er gospel: which is not another; but there be some that trouble you, and would pervert the gospel of

μετατίθεσθε ἀπὸ τοῦ καλέσαν-
τος ὑμᾶς ἐν χάριτι Χριστοῦ εἰς
ἔτερον εὐαγγέλιον· ὃ οὐκ ἔστιν 7
ἄλλο, εἰ μή τινές εἰσιν οἱ ταράσ-

---

ition state. Compare iii. 1, 3, v. 4, 7, with iv. 9, " turn," or 'are turning,' ἐπιστρέφετε, 20, v. 1, 10. No contradiction is hereby implied, as the Apostle's feelings at the moment of writing the respective portions, and the degree and extent of erroneous views embraced by various members of the Galatian church, will readily account for his varied language. It is probable that, if he had here intended to mark an absolutely completed apostasy to Judaism, he would have employed the aorist or perfect tense rather than the present. The same verb in the form of a middle partici-ple occurs in 2 Macc. vii. 24, where Antiochus makes lavish promises to the youngest of the seven Hebrew brothers who suffered martyrdom for their religion, " if he would *turn* from the laws of his fathers :" μεταθέμενον ἀπὸ τῶν πατρίων νόμων.

" Him that called you :" that is, God, who is uniformly represented as calling men to the Gospel. See the texts referred to in the latter part of the note on Heb. iii. 1 ; to which others might also be added.—" To an-other Gospel :" This refers to the *removal*, not to the *calling*. Ἕτερον, whence is derived in part our word *heterodox*, probably expresses the erroneous character of this so called Gospel in contrast with the true. This is not a necessary, but only an admissible sense of the word. Thus in 1 Tim. i. 3, ἑτεροδιδασκαλεῖν is used in the sense of teaching *false* doctrine.

7. " Which is not another," ἄλλο· That is, it is not truly another Gospel in the proper sense of the term ; it is no message of good tidings, however favorably you may regard it ; it perverts the genuine Gospel, and is therefore untrue. " But," εἰ μή· This is explained by Tyndale and Cranmer in connection with what precedes, thus : " Which is nothing else but that there be some," etc. Locke also gives this view in his paraphrase : " Which is not owing to anything else, but only this, that ye are troubled by a certain sort of men, who would overturn the Gospel of Christ." To the same purpose Olshausen, following Grotius and others : " Your apostasy is or consists in nothing else, than that you have allowed yourselves to be led astray." But this translation is too harsh, not to say feeble, to be admitted. Our English version, "but," makes the Greek particles εἰ μή equivalent to ἀλλά, which is not sustained by usage. The only passage where they may seem to have this sense is 1 Cor. vii. 17, and there they are best translated literally, *if not ;* meaning, if the conversion of the unbelieving married party should not take place, even in this case, " as God hath dis-tributed," etc. Perhaps, in this text of Galatians, the connection is with the first word of the preceding verse. The Apostle may begin by declar-

σοντες ὑμᾶς καὶ θέλοντες με-
ταστρέψαι τὸ εὐαγγέλιον τοῦ
8 Χριστοῦ. Ἀλλὰ καὶ ἐὰν ἡμεῖς
ἢ ἄγγελος ἐξ οὐρανοῦ εὐαγγελί-
ζηται ὑμῖν παρ' ὃ εὐηγγελισά-
9 μεθα ὑμῖν, ἀνάθεμα ἔστω. Ὡς
προειρήκαμεν καὶ ἄρτι πάλιν
λέγω, εἴ τις ὑμᾶς εὐαγγελίζεται
παρ' ὃ παρελάβετε, ἀνάθεμα
10 ἔστω. Ἄρτι γὰρ ἀνθρώπους
πείθω, ἢ τὸν Θεόν; ἢ ζητῶ

Christ. But though we, or an an- 8
gel from heaven, preach any other
gospel unto you than that which
we have preached unto you, let
him be accursed. As we said be- 9
fore, so say I now again, If any
man preach any other gospel unto
you than that ye have received, let
him be accursed. For do I now 10
persuade men, or God? or do I seek
to please men? for if I yet pleased

---

ing his wonder at their hasty transformation, and then introduce as an explanation of the strange fact and as a sort of apology for the perverts; " only there are some that trouble you, and are eager to overturn the Gospel." Olshausen maintains this to " be totally unallowable, because of the indicative (in ver. 6,) which cannot possibly mean, *I should won-der*," etc. But this translation of θαυμάζω is not necessary in order to sustain such a connection. *Only* has a corrective force. It is as if the writer had said, ' I wonder,—and yet on reflection, I need not very greatly wonder, when I consider the circumstances in which you have been thrown.' Θέλοντες here denotes the bent of the mind, as it also often does elsewhere.

8, 9. The Apostle puts an extreme hypothetical case in order to express in the strongest possible way his abhorrence of such erroneous teaching as the Galatians had been subjected to. Comp. Rom. viii. 38, where angels are introduced among a group of beings who are represented as unable to separate the true Christian from the love of God. In neither case is their actual agency to be inferred.—" Accursed:" that is, an object devoted to destruction. See the note on Rom. ix. 3.—Παρά is best trans-lated *contrary to*, as it is used in Rom. xi. 24.—The next verse repeats the same general declaration for the sake of emphasis. The words, " as we said before," may refer to those in the immediately preceding verse. But from the use of the term "now," it is not improbable that they are in con-tradistinction to what the Apostle had said to the Galatians at a previous visit.

10. "For," γάρ· Here, as generally in the New Testament, this par-ticle is illative. Its force and connection are as follows : This declaration is in harmony with my conduct and habits; " for do I now," since my con-version to the Gospel of Christ, etc. "Persuade:" That is, sooth, con-ciliate the favor of, as the original word is used in Acts xii. 20, ' having soothed or conciliated Blastus,' and 1 Sam. xxiv. 8, (7, Eng. Tr.) ' David soothed his men.' There is evidently a reference to the charges of un-

men, I should not be the servant of
11 Christ. But I certify you, brethren, that the gospel which was
preached of me, is not after man.
12 For I neither received it of man,
neither was I taught *it*, but by the
13 revelation of Jesus Christ. For ye
have heard of my conversation in
time past in the Jews' religion,
how that beyond measure I persecuted the church of God, and
14 wasted it; and profited in the
Jews' religion above many my
equals in mine own nation, being

ἀνθρώποις ἀρέσκειν; εἰ γὰρ ἔτι
ἀνθρώποις ἤρεσκον, Χριστοῦ δοῦλος οὐκ ἂν ἤμην. Γνωρίζω δὲ 11
ὑμῖν, ἀδελφοί, τὸ εὐαγγέλιον τὸ
εὐαγγελισθὲν ὑπ' ἐμοῦ ὅτι οὐκ
ἐστι κατὰ ἄνθρωπον· οὐδὲ γὰρ 12
ἐγὼ παρὰ ἀνθρώπου παρέλαβον
αὐτὸ οὔτε ἐδιδάχθην, ἀλλὰ δι'
ἀποκαλύψεως Ἰησοῦ Χριστοῦ.
Ἠκούσατε γὰρ τὴν ἐμὴν ἀνα- 13
στροφήν ποτε ἐν τῷ Ἰουδαϊσμῷ,
ὅτι καθ' ὑπερβολὴν ἐδίωκον τὴν
ἐκκλησίαν τοῦ θεοῦ καὶ ἐπόρθουν
αὐτήν· καὶ προέκοπτον ἐν τῷ 14

steadiness, inconsistency, and perhaps duplicity, which had been brought
against the Apostle. If, says he, my object still were to please men, as it
was in my former unconverted condition. This seems to be implied in
the particle " yet." The next clause has been interpreted by some in this
way : 'I should not be a servant of Christ, I should not have put myself in
such a position.' But it is vastly preferable to explain it thus : 'I should
not be a true servant of Christ.'

11. De Wette characterises the portion that immediately follows to
the end of the second chapter as the 'Apologetic Section,' and the subsequent one to v. 12, as the ' Polemic.'

" After (or, according to) man :" that is, in character with human weakness and infirmity. This is the general, though not invariable, meaning
of the phrase. See the note on Rom. iii. 5, p. 46.

12. It is hardly to be supposed that St. Paul intends to say, that he
derived all his knowledge of the facts and truths of Christianity directly
from divine revelation. He must have gone to Jerusalem early in life,
for he says he was brought up there : Acts xxii. 3. Educated in that city
under the distinguished Gamaliel, it is most probable that he was in some
degree acquainted with the claims of Jesus, and with some of the alleged
facts by which they were sustained, and perhaps also some of the doctrines
which he avowed. It is further probable, that some portion of his knowledge of the Gospel was obtained from earlier Christian converts. He
seems here to have in view its prominent and fundamental principles, the
divine Messiahship of Jesus and the doctrines necessarily connected therewith, which were divinely communicated to him immediately after his
miraculous call, and perhaps during the three days which preceded his
baptism, and probably also in visions, such as that mentioned in Acts xxii.
17, 18, and on other occasions, when " God revealed " to his Apostle " by
the Spirit :" 1 Cor. ii. 10, 12, xiv. 6, 2 Cor. xii. 1, Eph. iii. 3.

'Ιουδαϊσμῷ ὑπὲρ πολλοὺς συνηλι-
κιώτας ἐν τῷ γένει μου, περισσοτ-
έρως ζηλωτὴς ὑπάρχων τῶν πατ-
15 ρικῶν μου παραδόσεων. ῞Οτε
δὲ εὐδόκησεν ὁ Θεός, ὁ ἀφορίσας
με ἐκ κοιλίας μητρός μου καὶ καλ-
έσας διὰ τῆς χάριτος αὐτοῦ,
16 ἀποκαλύψαι τὸν υἱόν αὐτοῦ

more exceedingly zealous of the
traditions of my fathers. But 15
when it pleased God, who separated
me from my mother's womb, and
called *me* by his grace, to reveal 16
his Son in me, that I might preach
him among the heathen; immediately I conferred not with flesh

---

15. After mentioning his former course of life, as a virulent persecutor of God's church and a zealous adherent to Jewish traditions, he introduces the fact of his conversion and call to the ministerial office. "Separated me from my mother's womb:" It has been suggested that this may refer to providential arrangements whereby he was, from very early life, so trained as best to prepare him for that position in which God intended to place him. The mode of conveying this thought has been compared with language in Ps. lviii. 3: "The wicked are estranged *from the womb;* they go astray, *as soon as they be born*, speaking lies." But no doubt it expresses the divine *purpose* in relation to the Apostle from his very birth, God being said to do what he determines, as in Rom. ix. 23. Thus it is said of Jeremiah, "*Before thou camest forth out of the womb* I sancti-fied thee, and I ordained thee a prophet unto the nations:" i. 5. Also in the person of the Messiah: "The Lord hath called me *from the womb, from the bowels of my mother* hath he made mention of my name;" xlix. 1.

16, 17. "To reveal his Son in me:" Some commentators translate the Greek ἐν ἐμοί *by me*, and explain the whole clause thus: to make known his Son by my means. But this is quite improbable. The revela-tion spoken of is plainly distinguished from the preaching of the Gospel by the Apostle, as the next clause shows; and preceded it, as the neces-sary means preparatory to this object. The author evidently refers to what is said in ver. 12, "by revelation of Jesus Christ." To reveal his Son in him is to make known to him the Son's character, offices and course of action towards men, in other words, his Gospel. In a similar sense we have the phrase in Matt. xi. 27, "to whom the Son will reveal him," the Father; that is, make his character and dispensations to his creatures to be known and appreciated. Thus also to "preach Christ" in Acts viii. 5, and Col. i. 28, is equivalent to preaching his Gospel.—"Flesh and blood" is a phrase for man. It either describes him as he appears, or is expressive of his weakness or imperfection. In Matt. xvi. 17, it stands in contra-distinction to what is divine.—On his miraculous call, the Apostle neither advised with human counsellors nor repaired to Jerusalem to receive directions from the earlier Apostles, but went without delay to Arabia. This is the most natural connection of the word "immediately."

2

17 and blood: neither went I up to
Jerusalem to them which were
apostles before me; but I went
into Arabia, and returned again

ἐν ἐμοί, ἵνα εὐαγγελίζωμαι αὐτὸν
ἐν τοῖς ἔθνεσιν, εὐθέως οὐ προσ-
ανεθέμην σαρκὶ καὶ αἵματι, οὐδὲ 17
ἀνῆλθον εἰς Ἰεροσόλυμα πρὸς
τοὺς πρὸ ἐμοῦ ἀποστόλους, ἀλλ'
ἀπῆλθον εἰς Ἀραβίαν, καὶ πάλιν

This journey to Arabia is entirely omitted in the narrative of St. Luke. He mentions St. Paul's preaching in the synagogues of Damascus immediately after his public profession of Christianity by baptism; the attempts of the Jews to destroy him; his escape and presence at Jerusalem: Acts ix. 20, 23—26. His going to Arabia must have preceded his visit to the holy city. To what particular part of this extensive region he went, and also what was the purpose of his journey thither, is uncertain. It has been conjectured by some expositors that he sought retirement, desiring opportunity for reflection and preparation of mind and heart for the exercise of the ministry. Olshausen remarks: "To me it appears most probable that St. Paul passed the longest time (of the three years,) in Arabia, because there he contemplated not teaching, but his own inward development. See Section 1st of the general introduction to St. Paul's Epistles, and in Acts ix. 20, et seq." It has also been supposed that much of the Apostle's knowledge of the Gospel was divinely communicated to him while in Arabia. It is surprising that so much positive assertion on matters utterly unknown should have been hazarded by writers eminent for learning and research. Thus Dr. Davidson tells us that "full and complete disclosures of the Gospel were made during his residence in Arabia. On the way to Damascus, a sudden and violent revolution had taken place in his ideas. Hence a calm interval was necessary for arranging them. The Old Testament, in its relation to Christianity, had to be studied. His mind had to be nurtured in the faith. He was separated therefore from intercourse with men, even with Christians; that he might be prepared, irrespectively of human teaching, for the labors of his life. In Arabia, where he continued the greater part of three years, he meditated on the discoveries made to him. There he was largely favored with divine disclosures. In that district, the doctrinal system, now denominated *the Pauline*, took hold of his mind and heart. In Arabia Paul was not a preacher of the Gospel in the sense he himself afterwards attached to the expression, and indeed according to its proper acceptation. He went through a process of training there for the purpose of preaching it. It was revealed to him in that place."* We naturally ask for some proof of these positive assertions; and the only possible

* Introduction to the New Testament, vol ii., pp. 79, 80.

18 ὑπέστρεψα εἰς Δαμασκόν. Ἔπει- unto Damascus. Then after three 18
τα μετὰ ἔτη τρία ἀνῆλθον εἰς years I went up to Jerusalem to
'Ιεροσόλυμα ἱστορῆσαι Πέτρον, see Peter, and abode with him
καὶ ἐπέμεινα πρὸς αὐτὸν ἡμέρας

---

reply is, that the Scripture affords us not a particle of information on the subject. It is all conjectural, or, at the best, inferential and uncertain.

After such positive declarations respecting matters of which it is impossible to be certain, it is refreshing to find such an inquirer as Ellicott, inclining as he does to the same general view, expressing himself in the doubtful language of one who knows that sufficient data for absolute assertions cannot be obtained. "The object of this abode in Arabia, *probably* religious meditation, (is a) contested point. That St. Paul might have preached in Arabia is not improbable; but his primary object in going there *seems* to have been meditation and seclusion:" p. 15.

But if St. Paul, immediately after his conversion, were in a fit mental and spiritual condition to preach the Gospel at Damascus, and to confound the Jews of that city by proving Jesus to be the true Messiah, the preparations and divine instructions spoken of had already been attained. In all probability he went to Arabia because a favorable opportunity presented itself there for making known the Gospel; and this seems to be intimated by the connection in which the statement here occurs. When God, who had designed him for the ministry, made him rightly acquainted with the truths of the Gospel, in order that he might announce them to the Gentiles, he lost no time in seeking human counsel or sanction, but went immediately to Arabia. The impression most naturally given by this representation is, that he went to preach the Gospel.

18. From Arabia the Apostle returned to Damascus. Three years after he went to Jerusalem. It is doubtful whether this period is to be reckoned from his conversion or from his return from Arabia. The latter is preferred by Koppe, and Borger also favors it, chiefly on account of the particle "then," which generally connects a narrative with what immediately precedes. But as no account is given of his pursuits and course of life during these three years, as there probably would have been if they had been spent at Damascus in preaching the Gospel, and as the period of his conversion must have been with him a very important epoch, it is most probable that they are to be dated from that event. This reference to a period of "three years" is probably in designed contrast with the word "immediately" in ver. 16. The Apostle is particular in stating both the object which he had in view, and the brief space of time that he remained in the capital. He went simply to form an acquaintance with Peter, the distinguished Apostle to the Jews, not to obtain authoritative sanction for an office which had been divinely imparted to him. He

| 19 fifteen days. But other of the apostles saw I none, save James | δεκαπέντε· ἕτερον δὲ τῶν ἀποσ- τόλων οὐκ εἶδον, εἰ μὴ Ἰάκωβον | 19 19 |

went, not to be instructed in the true nature of the Gospel, which he already knew by revelation, and therefore remained only the short space of of fifteen days.

19. Besides Peter he saw no other Apostle but "James the Lord's brother." Commentators are divided in opinion on the question whether there were three Apostles of the name of James or only two. Those who adopt the latter view affirm that James the Lord's brother, who is also distinguished by the appellation of the just, and known in early ecclesiastical history as the first bishop of Jerusalem, was identical with James the less, the son of Alphæus. The only other Apostle of the name will be the son of Zebedee, who was put to death by Herod Agrippa I. Acts xii. 2. But others maintain that the James here spoken of, the Lord's brother and bishop of Jerusalem, who also wrote the canonical Epistle, was a different person from both the original Apostles. So Koppe in loc., and Kuinoel on Matt. x. 2 ; also Rosenmüller on James i. 1, who says that the James of Matt. xiii. 55, was a different person from the son of Alphæus. Olshausen is of the same opinion, arguing from John vii. 5, that "the identification of our Lord's brother with the son of Alphæus is inadmissible." Bishop White also supports the same view in his Lectures on the Catechism, pp. 431, 432. On the other hand, Borger defends at some length the theory that there were only two of the name, and consequently identifies the son of Alphæus with the Lord's brother. The whole subject is examined in detail by Julius Pott, in his Prolegomena to the Epistle of St. James, prefixed to his Commentary and published in the ninth volume of Koppe's New Testament, Göttingen, 1816, pp. 63–90. To this author I refer the reader who desires to see what may be said on both sides. If one of our Lord's brothers belonged to the number of the original twelve Apostles, it seems inexplicable that St. John should make the remark, "neither did his brethren believe in him," (vii. 5,) without noting the prominent exception. The Lord's brother may mean either a son of Joseph and Mary, or a son of Joseph by a former wife, or a cousin of the Lord, as the Hebrew use of the term for brother would admit the last exposition as well as the others. James is mentioned as bishop of Jerusalem by Eusebius,* and what is here and elsewhere said of him agrees entirely with the statement. In ii. 9, he is spoken of, along with Peter and John, as a distinguished Apostle. In ii. 12, "certain persons" are said to have "come from" him to Antioch. At the Council of Jerusalem he appears also as a prominent character : Acts xv. 13, 19. Paul, with his companions, goes to him to communicate

* Hist. Eccles. Lib. ii. cap. 23.

20 τὸν ἀδελφὸν τοῦ κυρίου. Ἃ δὲ
γράφω ὑμῖν, ἰδοὺ ἐνώπιον τοῦ
21 Θεοῦ, ὅτι οὐ ψεύδομαι. Ἔπειτα
ἦλθον εἰς τὰ κλίματα τῆς Συρίας
22 καὶ τῆς Κιλικίας. Ἤμην δὲ
ἀγνοούμενος τῷ προσώπῳ ταῖς
ἐκκλησίαις τῆς Ἰουδαίας ταῖς ἐν
Χριστῷ, μόνον δὲ ἀκούοντες
23 ἦσαν, ὅτι ὁ διώκων ἡμᾶς ποτε

the Lord's brother.   Now the 20
things which I write unto you,
behold, before God, I lie not.   Af- 21
terwards I came into the regions
of Syria and Cilicia; and was un- 22
known by face unto the churches
of Judea which were in Christ;
but they had heard only, That he 23
which persecuted us in times past,

"what God had wrought among the Gentiles by his ministry:" xxi. 19. Apart from ancient historical accounts, these particulars indeed prove nothing; but they agree exactly with the view of the ecclesiastical position of St. James as stated by the early writers. According to the minute account given by Hegesippus, he suffered martyrdom shortly before the siege of Jerusalem.*

This visit to Jerusalem is generally considered as the same with that mentioned in Acts ix. 26–28, and the opinion is very naturally suggested by a comparison of the two statements. The only plausible objection to it is that St. Paul expressly limits the number of the Apostles whom he there saw to Peter and James, while St. Luke states that " Barnabas brought him to the Apostles." But this statement is in general terms. The number of Apostles then at Jerusalem to whom St. Paul was introduced is not defined. The historian may not have been informed on this point. If there were but two, the plural would still be appropriate; and possibly others, besides the original twelve, may have been present to whom the appellation of Apostles had been applied. These, along with the other two, may be intended in the Acts, and the remark in the Epistle be limited to those originally appointed.

20. The author finds it necessary to make a strong asseveration of the truth of his statements, on account of the hostility and calumnies of his opponents.

21. At Jerusalem the Hellenists with whom Paul had disputed attempted to kill him. He therefore left the city and went to Cæsarea and thence to Tarsus. The Apostle omits some particulars which are stated by St. Luke. Syria is here most probably to be taken in the more enlarged meaning, comprehending the region of country lying between the mountains Taurus and Amanus on the north, and the Euphrates and Mediterranean on the east and west. Tarsus, the birth place of St. Paul, was in Cilicia. · See Acts ix. 29, 30, and xi. 25.

22, 23. The remarks here made seem to allude to the topic on which the mind of the Apostle evidently dwelt. He was personally unknown

* In Eus. ubi sup.

now preacheth the faith which | νῦν εὐαγγελίζεται τὴν πίστιν,
24 once he destroyed. And they glo- | ἥν ποτε ἐπόρθει · καὶ ἐδόξαζον 24
rified God in me. | ἐν ἐμοὶ τὸν Θεόν.

II.   Then, fourteen years after, I | 'Έπειτα διὰ δεκατεσσάρων 1
went up again to Jerusalem with | ἐτῶν πάλιν ἀνέβην εἰς 'Ιεροσό-
Barnabas, and took Titus with *me* | λυμα μετὰ Βαρνάβα, συμπαρα-

---

to the Christian churches of Judea.   They had merely heard that the raging persecutor had become a defender of the faith.   Had he obtained his knowledge of the Gospel from the leaders of the church at Jerusalem, or applied for their sanction of his Apostolic authority, the churches of Judea could hardly have been so little acquainted with him.

ii. 1.   Several events in the Apostle's life are here omitted, some of which are supplied in the Acts.   Barnabas seeks him at Tarsus and brings him to Antioch, where they remain a whole year.   On the prediction of a famine by Agabus, the Christians of the vicinity send relief to those in Judea, and as their agents, these two Apostles visit Jerusalem a second time : Acts xi. 25–30.   (The first visit is mentioned in Acts ix. 26.) They returned to Antioch, and were divinely sent to preach to the Gentiles : xii. 25, xiii. 2, 3.   Having accomplished this mission, they returned again to Antioch : xiv. 26.   Here a dispute having arisen respecting the obligation of the Jewish ritual law, they are sent as a delegation to Jerusalem, where they meet the council consisting of the Apostles and elders and the church : xv. 22.   It is this visit to Jerusalem of which St. Paul here speaks, being the third.   The second just referred to in the Acts, he omits.   A fourth visit to Jerusalem is spoken of in Acts xviii. 21, as intended to be made, and a fifth is mentioned in xxi. 17.—After writing this, I find that Howson has given this same view of the respective visits to Jerusalem.   See his able note in vol. I. pp. 244–252, Eng. Edit.

The reader who may desire to see the views of the principal German critics on the question, whether the journey mentioned in ii. 1 of this Epistle is that of Acts xi. 30 or of xv. 2–4, is referred to De Wette's examination of it on pp. 21—25.

It is uncertain whether these fourteen years are to be computed from the date of his conversion or from the time of his leaving Jerusalem after his interview with Peter and James.   Koppe and Borger prefer the latter, arguing from the use of the expressions "then" and "after."   Διά occurs in this sense in Mark ii. 1, "after some days ;" in Acts xxiv. 17, "after many years ;" and also in Deut. ix. 11, where the literal translation of the Hebrew is, "at the end of forty days," &c.   Olshausen dates "from the conversion of St. Paul :" p. 31.   It is difficult to settle these chronological points in the Apostle's biography, as the data are not sufficiently definite.

2 λαβὼν καὶ Τίτον· ἀνέβην δὲ
κατὰ ἀποκάλυψιν, καὶ ἀνεθέμην
αὐτοῖς τὸ εὐαγγέλιον, ὃ κηρύσσω
ἐν τοῖς ἔθνεσι, κατ' ἰδίαν δὲ
τοῖς δοκοῦσι, μήπως εἰς κενὸν
3 τρέχω ἢ ἔδραμον. Ἀλλ' οὐδὲ
Τίτος ὁ σὺν ἐμοί, Ἕλλην ὤν,

also. And I went up by revela- 2
tion, and communicated unto them
that gospel which I preach among
the Gentiles; but privately to them
which were of reputation, lest by
any means I should run, or had
run, in vain. But neither Titus, 3

---

2. St Paul's statement that he undertook the journey to Jerusalem in consequence of a revelation to that effect, is not at all inconsistent with his having been appointed a delegate along with Barnabas. The appointment thus received the sanction of a divine direction.—Τοῖς δοκοῦσι is equivalent to τῶν δοκούντων εἶναί τι of ver. 6, and is very properly translated "to them of reputation." Theophylact explains it by "the great, the honorable."* Erasmus in loc. gives the same meaning, iis qui erant in pretio, those who were in high estimation; and Grotius quotes a passage from Euripides,† who contrasts δοκούντων with ἀδοξούντων, the noble with those of no repute. Borger also shows, from Porphyry and Philostratus in his life of Apollonius of Tyana, that this is a legitimate meaning of the word. See him in loc. and also on ver. 6.

The reason which induced the Apostle to state privately to these distinguished personages the general tenor of his preaching is expressed in the latter clause of the verse: "lest I should run or had run in vain;" that is, lest his efforts in attempting to spread the Gospel should be thwarted or made ineffective. Comp. Phil. ii. 16, "that I have not run in vain, neither labored in vain." It was prudent on his part to explain to those Apostolic men his views of the Gospel and his manner of proclaiming it, in order to secure their hearty approval and recommendation, which would have operated as a passport to the Apostle of the Gentiles.

3–5. It is proper to examine these three verses together, because their true meaning depends considerably upon the question whether οἷς οὐδέ (" to whom no, not,") in ver. 5 are genuine. Although these words are wanting in some important ancient authorities, yet the best critics regard them as authentic. Koppe is disposed to reject them. He thinks that the construction flows along the more readily without them, the particle δέ in ver. 4, which is rendered " and " in our translation, retaining its more usual adversative signification but, and the words "compelled" and "gave place" or yielded in vs. 3 and 5 making a suitable contrast. He supposes St. Paul to mean that Titus was not indeed compelled to be circumcised, but that on prudential considerations he himself voluntarily yielded to the

---

* Opera Omnia, Tom. ii. p. 333, Venet. 1775.
† Hecuba, 294, 295.

who was with me, being a Greek,	ἠναγκάσθη περιτμηθῆναι. Διὰ 4
was compelled to be circumcised:	δὲ τοὺς παρεισάκτους ψευδαδέλ-
4 and that because of false brethren	φους, οἵτινες παρεισῆλθον κατα-
unawares brought in, who came in	σκοπῆσαι τὴν ἐλευθερίαν ἡμῶν,
privily to spy out our liberty	ἣν ἔχομεν ἐν Χριστῷ Ἰησοῦ, ἵνα

occasion and circumcised him. He adduces the case of Timothy mentioned in Acts xvi. 3, and argues from the Apostle's practice of accommodating to Jewish rites when circumstances made it expedient, referring to what he did as recorded in Acts xxi. 26, and what he says in 1 Cor. ix. 19–23. The meaning which he gives is as follows: 'Titus was not *compelled* to be circumcised, but on account of the Judaizers I *yielded* for a space, and he was circumcised.' He attempts to remove the objections to his view which are drawn from the general tenor of the Epistle, and particularly from the immediate context; from the inconsistency of St. Paul's blaming so severely the Galatian Christians for adherence to the Jewish ritual, while he acknowledges that, on this most important occasion, he made such concessions himself; and also from his censuring St. Peter for similar conduct. But his replies are not satisfactory. He attaches too much importance to what he calls the different circumstances of the Apostle and the Galatians, as affording a reason in the one case which would not apply in the other. He says that St. Peter's behavior was contemptuous towards the Gentile Christians, which is mere assumption, while St. Paul's concession was made simply to avoid giving offence. It is impossible not to feel that the whole tenor of the doctrinal part of the Epistle, and particularly the connection of this portion, are at variance with the idea of any concession to Jewish ritualists. Besides, according to Koppe's view, it is hardly fair to say that the circumcision of Titus was not compulsory, inasmuch as it would have been forced upon the Apostle by the circumstances of the occasion. If he had assented to it, it would have been simply because he considered himself obliged to assent.

The internal evidence is therefore decidedly in favor of the disputed words, and the external authority is also highly respectable. With Storr, Borger, Olshausen, Neander, and other critics of great name, I cannot but regard them as genuine, and therefore proceed to examine the passage from this view.

There is a difficulty in the construction, as the 4th and 5th verses do not make a perfect sentence. Omitting the parenthesis, the literal translation is as follows: ' But on account of false brethren clandestinely introduced, to whom we did not yield by subjection for an hour, in order that the truth of the Gospel might be permanently established with you' ——. Something must be supplied to complete the sense. Borger suggests that the words οἷς οὐδέ may have been omitted by some early transcriber,

5 ·ἡμᾶς καταδουλώσουσιν· οἷς οὐδὲ   which we have in Christ Jesus,
πρὸς ὥραν εἴξαμεν τῇ ὑποταγῇ,   that they might bring us into
ἵνα ἡ ἀλήθεια τοῦ εὐαγγελίου   bondage : to whom we gave place 5

---

who presumed that the particle δέ implied something in contrast to what had preceded it, and therefore drew out such a meaning as Koppe defends, namely, that Titus was not compelled to be circumcised, but yet on account of the false brethren he was circumcised. As in this case it would be necessary to supply some word after "false brethren," εἴξαμεν, "we yielded," was chosen for that purpose, and, as οἷς οὐδέ would not accord with this construction, these words were stricken out. Their early omission, therefore, is attributable to a difficulty in the construction. The 4th verse may be connected with the second, and the particle δέ, *but*, be referred to ἀνέβην or ἀνεθέμην, "I went up," or "communicated." This connection, which is adopted by Borger after Stroth,* Rosenmüller,† and Storr,‡ removes the difficulty arising from the want of a perfect sentence. And moreover, it agrees well with the fact that St. Paul went to Jerusalem in consequence of false brethren, erroneous Judaizers, who endeavored to compel the Gentile converts to be "circumcised after the manner of Moses:" These false brethren may have been some of the persons referred to in Acts xv. 1, and the Apostle most probably alludes to efforts made by them at Antioch, where they clandestinely introduced themselves in order to subject the Gentile Christians to the law. Perhaps it is best to connect the particle δέ with ἀνεθέμην, as Borger suggests in a note, unless indeed the connection is with both verbs. This construction will appear the simpler, if we regard the 3rd verse as a parenthesis. The general view of the passage will be as follows : 'I made my journey to Jerusalem, and my communication of the Gospel as preached by me among the Gentiles ; (yet my companion Titus, although a Greek, was not obliged to be circumcised ;) but I made them on account of Judaizing teachers, to whom we did not succumb in the least, in order that the Gospel in its truth and integrity might be preserved for your benefit.'

De Wette agrees with Winer in explaining the clause "which we have in Christ Jesus," of "Paul, Barnabas, and Titus, and not of all evangelical Christians." But this is both unnecessary and inexpedient. The argument alleged that *you* in ver. 5 is in contrast with *us* in ver. 4, proves nothing of the sort. The liberty referred to certainly belongs to all true Christians. At the same time those of the Galatian and other churches who had

---

* In his Umschreibende Uebersetzung, Paraphrastic Translation and Exposition of some difficult passages in the Epistle to the Galatians: In the Repertorium für Biblische und Morgenländische Litteratur. Leip. 1779, vol. iv. p. 48.

† Scholia in loc.

‡ Opuscula Academica, Tubingæ, 1808, vol. iii. pp. 297, 298.

by subjection, no, not for an hour; that the truth of the gospel might 6 continue with you. But of those who seemed to be somewhat, whatsoever they were, it maketh no matter to me; God accepteth no man's person; for they who seemed *to be somewhat,* in conference added 7 nothing to me: but contrariwise, when they saw that the gospel of the uncircumcision was committed unto me, as *the gospel* of the cir- 8 cumcision *was* unto Peter; (for he that wrought effectually in Peter to the apostleship of the circumcision, the same was mighty in me

διαμείνῃ πρὸς ὑμᾶς. Ἀπὸ δὲ 6 τῶν δοκούντων εἶναί τι, ὁποῖοί ποτε ἦσαν, οὐδέν μοι διαφέρει· πρόσωπον Θεὸς ἀνθρώπου οὐ λαμβάνει· ἐμοὶ γὰρ οἱ δοκοῦντες οὐδὲν προσανέθεντο, ἀλλὰ τού- 7 ναντίον, ἰδόντες, ὅτι πεπίστευ- μαι τὸ εὐαγγέλιον τῆς ἀκροβυσ- τίας, καθὼς Πέτρος τῆς περιτο- μῆς, (ὁ γὰρ ἐνεργήσας Πέτρῳ εἰς 8 ἀποστολὴν τῆς περιτομῆς ἐνήρ- γησε καὶ ἐμοὶ εἰς τὰ ἔθνη,) καὶ 9 γνόντες τὴν χάριν τὴν δοθεῖσάν μοι, Ἰάκωβος καὶ Κηφᾶς καὶ Ἰωάννης, οἱ δοκοῦντες στῦλοι

imbibed the Judaizing error could have no claim to it. The very admission of the error detracted from their evangelical character.—De Wette objects also to the view just given, and says that the reference to or, to use his own expression, the "repetition" of ἀνέβην in ver. 2, is "arbitrary." He connects the 3rd and 4th vs., and gives to the δέ in the latter an 'emphatic' or determining signification, as in Rom. iii. 22 and Phil. ii. 8, translating thus: "Titus, although a Greek, was not compelled to be circumcised, *and truly* on account of false brethren," etc. This he regards as a reason why he was not compelled. The reader is left to form his own judgment. With παρεισῆλθον compare παρεισάξουσι in 2 Pet. ii. 1, and παρεισέδυσαν in Jude 4.—"For an hour:" Maimonides uses the same phrase to express a short space of time.*

6–10. "Of those who seemed to be somewhat:" Τι has here the same general meaning as in 1 Cor. iii. 7, where it is translated "anything," and the whole phrase is equivalent to that already explained in ver. 2. The intermediate part of the verse from "whatsoever" to "person" inclusive seems parenthetical, and the idea with which the verse begins is then resumed in a somewhat different form. In rhetorical language, the author employs an anacoluthon. St. Paul recognised the dignity of the Apostles with whom he conferred at Jerusalem, at the same time averring that, however great it was, it did not affect him, as "God is no respecter of persons." It has been thought by some commentators that there may be an allusion here to the regard and personal consideration which were paid by the Church in general to the early Apostles, and also

* Foundations of the Law, chap. ix. sect. 5.

εἶναι, δεξιὰς ἔδωκαν ἐμοὶ καὶ
Βαρνάβᾳ κοινωνίας, ἵνα ἡμεῖς
μὲν εἰς τὰ ἔθνη, αὐτοὶ δὲ εἰς τὴν
10 περιτομήν· μόνον τῶν πτωχῶν
ἵνα μνημονεύωμεν· ὃ καὶ ἐσπού-

toward the Gentiles;) and when 9
James, Cephas, and John, who
seemed to be pillars, perceived the
grace that was given unto me,
they gave to me and Barnabas the
right hands of fellowship; that we
should go unto the heathen, and
they unto the circumcision. Only 10
they would that we should remember the poor; the same which I

---

to their honorable position, in contradistinction to the suspicion and doubt-
fulness with which St. Paul was regarded by many, and also to his own
personal infirmities, to which he frequently alludes. These eminent
leaders of the Church "added nothing to" him; that is, they neither increased his knowledge of the Gospel nor endowed him with authority to
preach it. On the contrary, they welcomed him as a coadjutor and
brother, whose allotted field was the Gentile world, as the Jewish had
been assigned chiefly to certain others.

"Was committed to me:" according to invariable usage in the New
Testament, the translation should be, "I was intrusted with." See the
note on Rom. iii. 2.—"Uncircumcision" and "circumcision" are abstracts
put for concretes, meaning Gentiles and Jews: See Rom. ii. 26, iii. 30.
"Grace" here means the favor of being made an Apostle. Comp. Rom.
i. 5, and Eph. iii. 8.—According to the best supported reading James is
placed before the other two Apostles, probably because of his ecclesiastical position as Bishop of Jerusalem, and also, as Neander thinks,* on account of his influence among those Jewish Christians who preserved their
attachment to the law. Some authorities give the precedence to Peter,
substituting this name for Cephas; but this arrangement has much less
external support than the other, and seems to have arisen either from a desire to make this Apostle prominent, or to adapt his position here to that
in Matt. x. 2, Mark iii. 16, and Luke vi. 14.—"Pillars:" Thus Horace calls
Mæcenas, grande decus *columenque* rerum ;† and Maimonides distinguishes
Abraham as "the pillar of the world."‡ After ἡμεῖς the particle μέν
should be inserted, as it is supported by the best external authority. The remainder of the sentence is evidently elliptical, and the words *should go*, or
preach, or some other equivalent expression, is understood. Similar ellipses
occur in v. 13, and Rom. v. 18. The next verse is also probably elliptical, though it may be connected with the clause, "they gave the right

---

* Geschichte der Pflanzung, &c. Hamburg, 1832, p. 100, note 2.
† Carm. ii. 17, 5, and perhaps i. 35, 13.
‡ Treatise on Idolatry, chap. i. sect. 5, or in Jewish Rabbies, p. 211.

11 also was forward to do. But when
Peter was come to Antioch, I
withstood him to the face, because
12 he was to be blamed. For before
that certain came from James, he
did eat with the Gentiles: but

δασα αὐτὸ τοῦτο ποιῆσαι. Ὅτε 11
δὲ ἦλθε Πέτρος εἰς Ἀντιόχειαν,
κατὰ πρώσωπον αὐτῷ ἀντέστην,
ὅτι κατεγνωσμένος ἦν. Πρὸ τοῦ 12
γὰρ ἐλθεῖν τινας ἀπὸ Ἰακώβου
μετὰ τῶν ἐθνῶν συνήσθιεν· ὅτε

---

hands of fellowship."—" The poor:" He refers to the poor Christians of
Judea for whom he made collections in several churches. See Acts xi.
29, 30, xxiv. 17, Rom. xv. 25, 2 Cor. viii. 4, ix. 1 et seq.

11–14. " When Peter was come to Antioch." Although this visit
is not narrated in the Acts, this is no serious objection to the supposition
that St. Peter had been at Antioch shortly before the difficulty stated in
the beginning of the 15th chapter.—Κατεγνωσμένος ἦν· " He was to be
blamed:" This translation may be traced to the vulgate, reprehensibilis
erat. It appears also in the older English versions, and is adopted by
several among the later interpreters. But the correct rendering is, ' he
was (or had been) blamed.' It is very probable that the conduct of St.
Peter had subjected him to censure on the part of Gentile converts, and
perhaps also of some among the more enlightened Jewish Christians.
Ellicott rejects this translation, but his own differs only in words. " The
meaning, ' reprehensionem incurrerat,' (Win.) or, still worse, ' he was to
blame,' (Peile,) rests, apparently, on no authority. The only tenable
translations are, he had been condemned, or he had been accused. Of these,
the former seems best to suit the context. As St. Peter's conduct had
generally been condemned by the sounder body of Christians at Antioch,
St. Paul as the representative of the anti-Judaical party, feels himself authorised publicly to rebuke him." As this was not a judicial condemna-
tion, but only that of general sentiment, Ellicott's meaning would seem
to be exactly equivalent to Winer's. It may be added, that St.
Paul's feeling himself authorised to rebuke must not be placed upon the
ground here stated, but simply upon that of right and duty.—" Before
that certain came from James:" These are probably the persons who
are said in the parallel places of Acts xv. 1, 24, to " have come down
from Judea," and "from us." Here they are said to have come from
James, inasmuch as he was head of the mother Church at Jerusalem. The
reason of our Apostle's opposition to St. Peter is too plain to be mistaken.
The conduct of the latter was insincere and culpable. He altered his
usual mode of living and his ordinary associations, refusing to continue
to mingle freely with the Gentiles as heretofore, through an improper desire to please those Jewish converts who were bigoted legalists. This
example of a man so distinguished seduced many other Jewish converts,
and even Barnabas himself. It is for blameworthy conduct that he is

δὲ ἦλθον, ὑπέστελλε καὶ ἀφώ-
ριζεν ἑαυτόν, φοβούμενος τοὺς
13 ἐκ περιτομῆς. Καὶ συνυπεκρί-
θησαν αὐτῷ καὶ οἱ λοιποὶ Ἰουδαῖοι, ὥστε καὶ Βαρνάβας συναπ-
ήχθη αὐτῶν τῇ ὑποκρίσει. Ἀλλ᾽

when they were come, he withdrew and separated himself, fearing them which were of the circumcision. And the other Jews 13
dissembled likewise with him; in-
somuch that Barnabas also was
carried away with their dissimu-

censured, not for error of opinion. Locke is altogether mistaken in the remark he makes on Rom. xvi. 25, that "St. Peter would not have incurred St. Paul's reproof, if he had been as clear as St. Paul was" on the doctrine of "the law of Moses being abolished by the death of Christ." Had he entertained doubts on this point, he would have been less censurable. It is not imperfect or erroneous views, but insincere behavior for which he is blamed; because he did not pursue the course of Christian simplicity, and evangelical truth and liberty. St. Paul had probably another motive for calling the attention of the Galatian Christians to his censure of St. Peter; namely, to show them that, so far from being indebted to the Apostles for his knowledge of the Gospel or authority as a commissioned minister thereof, he did not scruple plainly and openly to charge one of the most distinguished of them with insincerity, when the impropriety of his conduct jeoparded the truth. The assumption of such a right showed a consciousness that he " was not a whit behind the very chief of the Apostles :" 2 Cor. xi. 5.

The conjecture that the Peter here mentioned was not the Apostle, but some other inferior person of the name, is unworthy of any confutation. It is first mentioned by Clement of Alexandria, and afterwards by Chrysostom as an unfounded opinion,* and is maintained by the Jesuit, Harduin. Calmet has refuted it at length in a dissertation, which may be found in the Bible de Vence, Tom. xv. pp. 705–726; also Deyling, in his Observationes Sacræ, P. II. pp. 520 et seq.—Still less worthy of confutation is an old opinion, that the two Apostles had a mutual understanding, the one not intending to censure the other, who knew that the harsh language was designed merely for effect on the Jewish devotees, whom St. Paul wished to withdraw from their overweening attachment to the ritual law. This view is given by Chrysostom in the homily before referred to, sections 4, 7, 17, 18. Such representations are injurious to the religious character of the Apostles, and show in their defenders a lamentable deficiency of a right sense of moral obligation, although they seem to have sprung from an over estimate of Apostolic divine guidance and infallibility. Jerome in loc.† supposes that the opposition of Paul to Peter on this occasion was nothing but a feint, and endeavors to

* Hom. in Galat. ii. 11. § 15, Opera Omnia, Edit. Bened. Paris. 1721, tom. iii. p. 874.
† Comment. in Gal., Opera, Edit. Martianay, Paris. 1649, tom. iv. fol. 243.

14 lation. But when I saw that they walked not uprightly according to the truth of the gospel, I said unto Peter before *them* all, If thou, being a Jew, livest after the manner of Gentiles, and not as do the Jews, why compellest thou the Gentiles

ὅτε εἶδον, ὅτι οὐκ ὀρθοποδοῦσι 14 πρὸς τὴν ἀλήθειαν τοῦ εὐαγγε- λίου, εἶπον τῷ Πέτρῳ ἔμπροσ- θεν πάντων· εἰ σὺ Ἰουδαῖος ὑπάρχων ἐθνικῶς ζῇς καὶ οὐκ Ἰουδαϊκῶς, πῶς τὰ ἔθνη ἀναγ-

---

vindicate the propriety of simulation by adducing the examples of Jehu and David in 2 Kings x. 18 et seq. and 1 Sam. xxi. 13–15. Augustin, in one of his letters to Jerome,* objects to such a representation of Scripture, and expresses his regret that an exposition of this sort should have been published. For more on this subject the reader is referred to the note of Erasmus.

14–17. There is a difference of opinion among the commentators re- specting the extent of the address made to St. Peter. Some limit it to the remainder of the verse. The Apostle will then resume his discourse to the Galatians with ver. 15. Others, among whom are Stroth and Olshausen, continue it to the end of the chapter. Others again, and in their view Neander concurs,† more judiciously close the address with the 17th verse, and consider the remainder of the chapter as addressed to the Galatian churches. Koppe, who adopts the first view, says that the one last mentioned is destitute of all probability, omni probabili ratione des- tituitur : on ver. 21. Borger, who rather favors the second, denies that there is any trace of the discourse turning to the Galatians. Both these assertions are rash. It may be impossible to determine positively where the address to the Apostle terminates and the epistolary discourse is re- sumed, but the third view seems more probable than either of the others. The first makes the address unnaturally short, and the second unnecessa- rily long. The contents of the portion designated in the third view, entirely harmonize, as we shall see, with the supposition that St. Peter is the party addressed, and the language—" we who are Jews by nature, even we" —is inapplicable to the Galatian converts, the larger proportion of whom were doubtless of Gentile extraction. The strong expression—" God forbid"—would be a suitable termination of the address, and what follows is quite in character with the former chapter and part of this, where the author vindicates himself from the charge of inconsistency. And it is certainly not unworthy of notice that the first person singular is employed both before the 15th and after the 17th verses, while throughout the inter- mediate portion, supposed to be addressed to St. Peter, the Apostle includes himself and uses the plural. And the particle " for," at the commencement

---

* Epist. ad Hieron. xl., Opera, Edit. Bened., Ant. 1700, tom. ii. p. 64.   † Ubi sup. pp. 186, 187.

15 κάζεις Ἰουδαΐζειν; Ἡμεῖς φύσει   to live as do the Jews? We *who* 15
Ἰουδαῖοι, καὶ οὐκ ἐξ ἐθνῶν ἁμαρ-   are Jews by nature, and not sinners
16 τωλοί· εἰδότες δέ, ὅτι οὐ δικαι-   of the Gentiles, knowing that a 16
οῦται ἄνθρωπος ἐξ ἔργων νόμου,   man is not justified by the works
ἐὰν μὴ διὰ πίστεως Ἰησοῦ Χρισ-   of the law, but by the faith of Jesus
τοῦ, καὶ ἡμεῖς εἰς Χριστὸν Ἰη-   Christ, even we have believed in
σοῦν ἐπιστεύσαμεν, ἵνα δικαιω-   Jesus Christ, that we might be

---

of the 18th verse, shows a logical connection of what follows with the early part of the chapter. I conclude, therefore, that this view is more probable than either of the others. Of course, as Olshausen remarks, we have not the identical words of St. Paul, but the substance of his observations.

Ζῇς, the present, may be used historically for the past, or express the ordinary practice of the Apostle. To live like Gentiles and not Jews, means to live without regard to the Jewish ritual law, living with such regard being denoted by the term Judaizing.—"Sinners of the Gentiles:" St. Paul does not imply that in their former condition they were not sinners; he means they were not devoted to a sinful course of life or idolatrous, as Gentiles in general were. See Eph. ii. 2, 3. In ver. 16 δέ should be introduced, as it is supported by strong external authority. The sense, however, will not be affected. If it be omitted, the 15th and 16th verses will be closely connected, and the translation run thus: 'We, Jews by nature and not sinners of the Gentiles, knowing,' etc. Its admission will not necessarily affect the construction, as the particle may be rendered either *and* or *but* without destroying the grammatical connection with what precedes. Still it would perhaps be simpler in this case to regard the former verse as a complete sentence, and to understand the substantive verb, thus: 'We (are) Jews by nature and not sinners of the Gentiles. But knowing,' etc.—Ἐκ in ver. 16 is used for διά, 'by, through,' as it is also in Rom. i. 17, iii. 20. If it be taken in the sense of 'from,' it can only refer to the instrumental source of justification. Ἐὰν μή is equivalent to *only*. See Matt. xii. 4, Luke iv. 26, 27, and Rev. xxi. 27, where εἰ μή has the same meaning, and does not mark an exception of certain persons among those before referred to.—The object of faith is here twice expressed by the simple genitive. For the other forms see the note on Rom. iii. 25, pp. 55, 56.

The general tenor of the address to St. Peter is as follows: 'If thou, a Jew, livest habitually without regard to the Jewish ritual law, why dost thou now, by accommodating to Jewish prejudice and avoiding intercourse with Gentiles, through thy example compel these to Judaize? Why require of them an observance of the Mosaic ritual, and shun those who do not observe it? We are by nature and education Jews, and not

justified by the faith of Christ, and
not by the works of the law: for
by the works of the law shall no
17 flesh be justified. But if, while we
seek to be justified by Christ, we
ourselves also are found sinners, *is*
therefore Christ the minister of sin ?

θῶμεν ἐκ πίστεως Χριστοῦ καὶ
οὐκ ἐξ ἔργων νόμου, διότι ἐξ ἔργων νόμου οὐ δικαιωθήσεται
πᾶσα σάρξ. Εἰ δὲ ζητοῦντες 17
δικαιωθῆναι ἐν Χριστῷ εὑρέθη-
μεν καὶ αὐτοὶ ἁμαρτωλοί, ἄρα
Χριστὸς ἁμαρτίας διάκονος ; μὴ

wicked and abandoned Gentiles. But, knowing that a man is not justified
by obedience to the law, but only by faith in Jesus Christ, even we have
believed in Christ in order to be justified by faith in him and not by
obedience to the law, for by such obedience justification is unattainable.
But if, while we thus seek to be justified through Christ, even we are
nevertheless found to be sinners, in the same condition as unconverted
Gentiles, not justified, not acceptable to God ; is then Christ the minister
of sin ? its agent and promoter ? He hath established this method of justification ; he hath commissioned us to publish it to the world. Is the sin
of originating and promulging an erroneous and inefficient system his ?
Such a conclusion is to be repelled with horror.'

The particular time of this interview is not so clearly stated as to
be absolutely certain. Neander connects it with St. Paul's visit to Antioch which is mentioned in Acts xviii. 22, when he supposes St. Peter to
have been there and the Jews from Jerusalem who are said, in Gal.
ii. 12, to have come from James. He allows, however, that the
period is uncertain.* Olshausen, too, although he does not attempt to
settle the time, places this collision of the two Apostles after the decision
of the council mentioned in Acts xv. His language is as follows : "Sub-
joined to the proceedings at the council of the Apostles is a remarkable
report on a later occurrence, on which we have no information at all from
any other source. St. Paul reports here that St. Peter, when remains
uncertain, had come to Antioch, and had at first held communion with the
Gentile Christians. Here St. Peter and Barnabas appear quite wavering,
and that in a highly important point, after a solemn decision of the council :" pp. 39, 40. Dr. Schaff also, in his learned and valuable history of
the Apostolic church, dissents . from the opinion of Augustin, Grotius,
Hug and Schneckenburger, who ' place this occurrence before the Apostolical Convention ;" because "this does not agree at all with the order of
events as described in the Epistle to the Galatians," which, " by placing
this event in immediate connection with the conference of the Apostles,
indicates that it occurred not long after."† De Wette also takes the same
view, remarking that it is against the context to suppose that St. Paul

* Ubi sup. pp. 184 et seq., and 187, note 1.
† Book I. § 70, p. 257.

18 γένοιτο. Εἰ γὰρ ἃ κατέλυσα,   God forbid. For if I build again the 18
ταῦτα πάλιν οἰκοδομῶ, παρα-   things which I destroyed, I make
19 βάτην ἐμαυτὸν συνιστάνω. Ἐγὼ   myself a transgressor. For I through 19
γὰρ διὰ νόμου νόμῳ ἀπέθανον,   the law am dead to the law, that I

---

here does not follow the order of time, but refers to something which
had taken place before. He admits, however, that some time must
have elapsed to allow for the reaction. So also Howson: "From the
order of narration in Galatians, it is most natural to infer that the
meeting at Antioch took place soon after the Council at Jerusalem."*

I cannot see much force in this reasoning. It presumes, what is by no
means certain, that the whole narrative in this chapter is in chronological
order; and this because the preceding statements do really occur in such
order. But it ought to be noted that in connection with those statements
the time is very definitely marked: See in i. 16, "immediately;" in
18, "after three years;" in 21, "afterwards;" in ii. 1, "then fourteen
years after." In this case, however, the circumstance is said to have
taken place "when Peter was come to Antioch;" and his previous conduct
is represented to have been practised "before that certain came from
James," statements which are quite indefinite. Now it would be perfectly
natural in St. Paul, after speaking of the council at Jerusalem, where his
Apostolical authority was recognised by the older Apostles, to go back to
the antecedent occurrence of his having objected to the conduct of St. Peter.
It appears to me very unlikely that "soon" or "not long after" the decision of the council in which he and Barnabas took so prominent a part,
they would have acted as is here stated. Notwithstanding the weight of
those learned authorities, therefore, I am compelled to think it more
probable that St. Peter and the Judaizers were at Antioch some time
before the meeting of the council at Jerusalem, and that the controversy
which the insidious attempts of the "false brethren" produced, led to the
delegation of Paul and Barnabas to attend that council. Thus the connection of the 4th verse with the 2nd receives confirmation. If it were certain, as it is only probable, that those who "came down from Judea"
(Acts xv. 1,) were the same persons who, in verse 12, are said to have
"come from James," the time of this dispute would evidently have been
before the council.

18, 19. The Apostle, having fully established his character for stead-
fastness of purpose and consistency of conduct, now very naturally adds:
'Were I to attempt to re-establish the Mosaic ritual law, the obligation of
which I have strenuously endeavored to dissolve, I should not only be
unworthy of confidence, but by the very act make myself an offender.'

* Chap. VII. vol. I. p. 288, note.

3

20 might live unto God. I am crucified with Christ: nevertheless I
live; yet not I, but Christ liveth
in me: and the life which I now
live in the flesh, I live by the faith
of the Son of God, who loved me,

ἵνα θεῷ ζήσω. Χριστῷ συνεσταύ- 20
ρωμαι· ζῶ δὲ οὐκέτι ἐγώ, ζῇ δὲ
ἐν ἐμοὶ Χριστός· ὃ δὲ νῦν ζῶ ἐν
σαρκί, ἐν πίστει ζῶ τῇ τοῦ υἱοῦ
τοῦ θεοῦ, τοῦ ἀγαπήσαντός με
καὶ παραδόντος ἑαυτὸν ὑπὲρ

Then, implying the denial of such inconsistency, he gives as a reason for
his abandonment of the law as a ground of justification : "I through the law
am dead to the law, that I might live unto God :" That the law here
denotes the Mosaic is not to be doubted, both from the context and also
from what is said elsewhere. "Through the law :" That is, in consequence
of its inadequacy to remove the moral and punitive consequences of sin.
Comp. Acts xiii. 39, Rom. iii. 20, iv. 15, viii. 3, Gal. iii. 10, 12, 23, 24.
"Am dead to the law :" For the use of the figurative term "dead," see
the note on Rom. vi. 2. St. Paul here represents himself as dead to the law,
just as he had represented the Roman converts in Rom. vii. 4–6, where see
the notes. It is as if he had said, 'My connection with the law as a means
by which justification might be expected, has been dissolved.' Thus he
says in ver. 21, 'If justification were attainable by the law, Christ's death
would have been unnecessary ;' and in iii. 21, 'If the law could have secured
for us the blessing of life, justification would have been obtained by it.'
See Rom. viii. 3, where the cause of its inability is ascribed to the flesh,
that is, human weakness and sinfulness. The Apostle's experience of the
character and operation of the law as producing a proper consciousness of
sin and illustrating its true nature, as becoming the occasion of exciting
the natural man in opposition to its precepts, as leaving him without
power to live a holy life, and as condemning him for transgression, had
shown him the law's inadequacy, and led him to Christ. See the discus-
sion in Rom. vii. 5–25, with the comment.—Stroth's exposition of this
phrase, "through the sacred books of the Jews," supposing a reference to
Ps. cxliii. 2, and another view which explains it of the Christian system,
"the perfect law of liberty," (James, i. 25 ;) are alike inconsistent with
the author's manner and habit of thought. There is no sufficient reason
to think that the Psalm is quoted at all. Similar language occurs repeat-
edly in St. Paul's writings.—"That I may live unto God :" that is, to his
glory, in a holy and useful Christian life. Comp. Rom. vi. 11, 13.

20, 21. It may be that the figure begun in ver. 19 is here carried out
in the excruciating kind of death, and that the Apostle merely intends to
strengthen the thought already given of his utter severance from the law
as a justifying instrumentality. Thus in Rom. vi. 4, he carries out the
same figure of death into that of burial. Still, it seems more probable
that he makes a transition from deadness to the law to his deadness also

21 ἐμοῦ. Οὐκ ἀθετῶ τὴν χάριν τοῦ
Θεοῦ· εἰ γὰρ διὰ νόμου δικαιοσ-
ύνη, ἄρα Χριστὸς δωρεὰν ἀπέθ-
ανεν.

and gave himself for me. I do not 21
frustrate the grace of God: for if
righteousness *come* by the law, then
Christ is dead in vain.

to everything worldly and sinful. This accords with the language in vi.
14, " By whom (Christ) the world is *crucified* to me and I unto the world."
Compare also v. 24, " They that are Christ's have *crucified* the flesh" ; and
Rom. vi. 6, " Our old man is *crucified* with him." It agrees too with the
clauses that follow, which express the internal divine life of the Christian,
and cannot be restricted to a mere abandonment of dependence on the
law. This divine life the Apostle ascribes to the inward influence of
Christ, who habitually operates in him as an abiding agent, and
through the means of a living faith.—῎Ο may be regarded as the object
of ζῶ, and the translation be, ' what I now live,' that is, ' the life that I
live ;' or it may be governed by κατά understood. Compare Rom. vi. 10,*
and other similar places.—The first clause of the last verse is a meiosis.
The meaning is, I sustain and establish the grace of God, that is, that
system of divine favor which, through faith in Christ, brings us into a
state of acceptance with God.—" In vain," δωρεάν· In other words, un-
necessarily, without reason. Compare John xv. 25 : " They hated me
without a cause," δωρεάν.

SECTION II.

Chap. III.

THE INCONSISTENCY AND FOLLY OF ABANDONING THE GOSPEL FOR THE LAW IN
ORDER TO OBTAIN JUSTIFICATION. THE COVENANT MADE BY GOD WITH
ABRAHAM AND HIS SPIRITUAL PROGENY NOT ANNULLED BY THE SUBSE-
QUENT LAW OF MOSES. THIS WAS ONLY DISCIPLINARY AND PREPARATORY
TO THE GOSPEL, WHICH EMBRACES WITHIN THE RANGE OF ITS BLESSINGS,
AND UNITES MOST INTIMATELY TOGETHER ALL CONDITIONS OF MEN.

III. Ὦ ἀνόητοι Γαλάται, τίς ὑμᾶς
ἐβάσκανε [τῇ ἀληθείᾳ μὴ πεί-
θεσθαι] ; οἷς κατ᾽ ὀφθαλμοὺς
Ἰησοῦς Χριστὸς προεγράφη ἐν

O foolish Galatians, who hath III.
bewitched you, that ye should not
obey the truth, before whose eyes
Jesus Christ hath been evidently

iii. 1. " Foolish :" ἀνόητοι· senseless, without consideration and reflection. Comp. Luke xxiv. 25. " Bewitched :" The Apostle thus expresses his
amazement at the foolish conduct of the Galatians, as if, to the imminent
danger of their ultimate ruin, they had been fascinated by some most in-

set forth, crucified among you? | ὑμῖν ἐσταυρωμένος. Τοῦτο μόν- 2
2 This only would I learn of you, Re- | ον θέλω μαθεῖν ἀφ' ὑμῶν· ἐξ
ceived ye the Spirit by the works of | ἔργων νόμου τὸ πνεῦμα ἐλάβετε,
the law, or by the hearing of faith?

---

explicable influence operating like a supposed charm. The use of the
terms merely implies deceit and cunning on the part of the false teachers,
and ignorance and simplicity in those whom they had beguiled. The
words, "that ye should not obey the truth," are probably spurious, as
they are wanting in the best ancient manuscripts and versions. They
appear to have been inserted from v. 7. The latter half of the verse is a
strong figure to denote how thoroughly, accurately, and graphically, the
Galatians had been instructed in the prominent doctrines of the Gospel,
and especially in those connected with Christ's death. The Apostle speaks
as if they had been made to gaze upon the crucified. The preposition in
προεγράφη expresses publicity, as it does also in Rom. iii. 25, not precedence in point of time. Οἷς may be connected with ἐν ὑμῖν and regarded as a Hebraism, equivalent to אֲשֶׁר־בָּכֶם, you among whom; literally, whom among you. But it is more natural to give the clause this construction : ' Before whose eyes Jesus Christ hath been graphically and
openly delineated (as if) crucified among you.' The words ἐν ὑμῖν have
been stricken out in several ancient authorities, being perhaps regarded as
pleonastic and unnecessary. But they are most probably genuine.

2. The Apostle puts a case which evidently arises from his strong feeling of the irrational and even silly procedure of the Galatians. It is the
reductio ad absurdum ; as if he had said : ' Answer me, I pray you, this
one question; I will trouble you with nothing else. From whence did
you receive the Holy Spirit, the divine agent who has dispensed his
miraculous gifts and ordinary grace among you? Did you receive his
influences from obedience to the Mosaic law, or from faith in the system
of the Gospel, made known to you by open proclamation, and thus heard
and accepted?' The word faith is certainly sometimes used by St. Paul
to express the Gospel itself, though not very often. Generally it denotes
the principle in the mind of the believer which leads him to embrace the
Gospel. And in this sense it is here and in the subsequent context employed. For, surely, as Borger very correctly remarks, an antithesis cannot lie between Abraham's faith, which was a personal quality, and Christianity, which is a religious system. There is a congruity between Abraham's faith and that here intended, and consequently the idea in each case
is that of believing. The phrase, "hearing of faith," may be illustrated by
referring to Isa. liii. 1, and Rom. x. 16, 17. In the last verse ἀκοή is
twice rendered in our English translation by "hearing," and in the preceding one by "report," marginal reading "preaching." In the prophet,

3 ἢ ἐξ ἀκοῆς πίστεως; Οὕτως ἀνό-
  ητοί ἐστε; ἐναρξάμενοι πνεύματι
4 νῦν σαρκὶ ἐπιτελεῖσθε; Τοσαῦτα
5 ἐπάθετε εἰκῇ; εἴγε καὶ εἰκῇ. Ὁ
  οὖν ἐπιχορηγῶν ὑμῖν τὸ πνεῦμα
  καὶ ἐνεργῶν δυνάμεις ἐν ὑμῖν,
  ἐξ ἔργων νόμου, ἢ ἐξ ἀκοῆς πίσ-
6 τεως;· Καθὼς Ἀβραὰμ ἐπί-
  στευσε τῷ Θεῷ, καὶ ἐλογίσθη
7 αὐτῷ εἰς δικαιοσύνην. Γινώσκετε
  ἄρα, ὅτι οἱ ἐκ πίστεως, οὗτοί

Are ye so foolish? having begun in 3
the Spirit, are ye now made perfect
by the flesh? Have ye suffered so 4
many things in vain? If it be yet
in vain. He therefore that minis- 5
tereth to you the Spirit, and worketh miracles among you, *doeth he it*
by the works of the law, or by the
hearing of faith? Even as Abra- 6
ham believed God, and it was accounted to him for righteousness.
Know ye therefore that they which 7
are of faith, the same are the child-

the corresponding term which the Septuagint has rendered by the same
Greek word, is שְׁמֻעָה, what is heard. This is "of faith," that is, it requires
faith. Thus it becomes clear that faith is the principle, and "hearing" or
"report," or, better than either, 'what is heard,' is its object. The meaning
of the phrase, therefore, is this: 'The doctrine or system which requires
faith, and which is embraced after having been heard.'

3. "The spirit" and "the flesh" are here contrasted. The former implies the excellence and superiority of the Gospel system; the latter
denotes what is inferior, external and carnal. See Essay on our Lord's
Discourse at Capernaum in John vi. pp. 101, 102.

4. Stroth, Olshausen and others, regard the last clause as conveying
this idea: 'if indeed it is nothing more than in vain,' if, by falling away
entirely from the faith, something 'worse do not befall you.' But it is
more natural to suppose that the Apostle intimates his hope that what the
Galatians had already endured for the Gospel would not eventually be in
vain; that they would recover from the spiritual declension into which
they had fallen, and be confirmed in their adherence to the true Gospel.

5-7. The idea in the 5th verse is equivalent to that in the 3d: 'The
spiritual officer whom God hath entrusted with the communication of the
Spirit to you and the performance of miracles among you, does not act
through obedience to the law, but through faith in the proclaimed and
heard system of the Gospel.' And this he immediately illustrates by the
example of Abraham who believed God, and was consequently justified.
What is here said to be "accounted to" the patriarch, is his faith; his justification resulted from this accounting. See Rom. iv. 2 et seq. and notes,
especially pp. 61-64.—"Know:" This is imperative, not indicative; for
the Apostle could not properly say of such persons as the Galatians, "ye
know." On the contrary, he calls on them to consider and attend to the
fact, that the faithful are Abraham's genuine children; and that whether
lineally derived from him or not. "They who are of faith:" In other

8 ren of Abraham. And the Scripture, foreseeing that God would
justify the heathen through faith,
preached before the Gospel unto
Abraham *saying,* In thee shall all

εἰσιν υἱοὶ ᾿Αβραάμ. Προϊδοῦσα 8
δὲ ἡ γραφή, ὅτι ἐκ πίστεως δι-
καιοῖ τὰ ἔθνη ὁ Θεός, προευηγ-
γελίσατο τῷ ᾿Αβραάμ· ὅτι ἐνευ-
λογηθήσονται ἐν σοὶ πάντα τὰ

words, believers. Compare "they who are of the law" in Rom. iv. 14,
and "they that are of Christ," in Gal. v. 24.—It is not a natural but a
spiritual descent which he has in view, and therefore he proceeds to make
the statement contained in the next verse.*

8. "The Scripture foreseeing:" That is here predicated of the Scripture which is intended of God. The rabbies employ similar language.
See Surenhusius, pp. 6, 7, and compare ver. 22, "the Scripture hath concluded," with Rom. xi. 32, "God hath concluded."—"Would justify:"
rather 'justifies.' The Greek is in the present tense.—"Preached the
Gospel:" In exact analogy with this declaration is that in Heb. iv. 2,
where see the note. Tyndale and Cranmer translate: "Showed before-
hand glad tidings unto Abraham." The quotation here made is taken
from the book of Genesis, where the promise is several times repeated.
See xii. 3, xviii. 18, xxii. 18, xxvi. 4, and xxviii. 14. In the first two
instances, and also in the last, the Niphal is employed; in the other two
the Hithpael. The result however is the same, the former being taken in
its ordinary passive sense, and the other retaining its usual reflexive meaning, 'shall regard themselves as blessed.' Thus also we find this same
form in Ps. lxxii. 17, where the Messiah is the subject, and the clause in
Genesis is probably quoted. The gloss of the Jewish commentator Rashe,
which formerly Le Clerc adopted, and with which the view of Jowett
agrees, is this: 'By thee all nations shall bless.' But this would require
the Hithpael invariably, and the correct rendering would be 'shall bless

---

* There are some extravagances so absurd as to be really unworthy of serious refutation; and yet
such is the influence of authority with multitudes, that they will read and acquiesce in anything that
may emanate from a favorite system or teacher, without taking the trouble to examine or even to think
whether it be susceptible of proof. It is this consideration and none other, which prevails upon me,
not without reluctance, to take notice of an interpretation of the phrase "Abraham's seed," which
appears in the Theological and Literary Journal for October, 1853, pp. 182, 185, 186, 188, 189, 191.
After hearing the author's affirmations, "that none but lineal descendants of Abraham are ever
denoted by that term;" that "there is not a solitary instance in which it is employed to mean believing Gentiles;" that of "all the seed" spoken of in Rom. iv. 16, that portion which is said to be "of
the faith of Abraham" denotes "part of his lineage living betwixt the date of the promise and the imposition of the law, or after the law was superseded by the Gospel;" we may well be prepared for any
extravagance. It might be amusing, were not every approximation to such feeling checked by the
melancholy seriousness of the consideration, that he even ventures to expound Rom. iv. 11, 12, where
Abraham is represented as the father of the uncircumcised believers as well as the circumcised, in
reference to "the myriads and probably millions of his offspring" *who were not of the* "*sex*" *to which*
"*only the sign was affixed*"! ! It is to be hoped that he felt some scruples in avowing such a
strange perversion of sober exposition, for he does qualify it by adding: "And there were periods,
there is reason to believe, when many of his male offspring also, who had faith, through the peculiar
condition of the nation or negligence of parents, were not circumcised."

9 ἔθνη. Ὥστε οἱ ἐκ πίστεως εὐλογ-   nations be blessed. So then they 9
   οῦνται σὺν τῷ πιστῷ ᾿Αβραάμ.   which be of faith are blessed with
10 Ὅσοι γὰρ ἐξ ἔργων νόμου εἰσίν,   faithful Abraham. For as many 10
   ὑπὸ κατάραν εἰσί· γέγραπται   as are of the works of the law are

---

himself,' as in Deut. xxix. 18, (19,) "he shall bless himself in his heart."
Besides, it is irreconcilable with the adjunct, "through thy seed," which
occurs in all the instances of the promise except the first two. This is
explanatory of the other phrase, "through thee." The only correct application of the repeated promise is that here made by St. Paul, namely, the
spiritual blessings which were intended to be conferred upon all nations or
families of mankind through the spiritual descendants of Abraham, and
immediately from the head, the most glorious of all, the divine Messiah.
With the texts above cited, compare Acts iii. 25, 26.

9. "So then:" As the spiritual blessings of the Gospel constituted the
principal portion of what was promised to Abraham on account of his
faith, the Apostle connects along with him the true Christian believer.
Both partake of the same blessings.—"*With* Abraham.:" That is, as he is.
Thus the Hebrew preposition *with* is used in Eccles. ii. 16 : 'The wise
man dieth as (literally *with*) the fool,' meaning, as well as he, death equally
happening to both.—"They that are of faith" is equivalent to 'believers.'
The same and similar phrases occur elsewhere. See Rom. iii. 26, and
note : p. 57.

10. The phrase, "of the works of the law," is of the same kind as that
just explained, only it expresses something more than mere connection
with the law, namely, dependence on it for acceptance with God; for this
the context requires. So the words, "they who are of the law," are used in
Rom. iv. 14, where see the note.—"Under the curse:" Literally, 'under
curse;' although the context shows what particular curse is here intended,
namely, that which by divine determination follows the transgression of
God's law.—The particle "for" is illative. The argument is that those
who depend upon the law for justification are subjected to the curse which
the law denounces against every one who in the slightest degree trans-
gresses any of its precepts; and it is valid on no other supposition than
this, that every fallen man is such a transgressor. This the Apostle may
well assume as a conceded point, "for there is no man that sinneth not :"
1 Kings viii. 46. The denunciation, therefore, applies to all mankind in
their fallen condition, and irrespective of the Gospel. This is briefly but
clearly expressed by Justin Martyr, who quotes to this effect these words
of Moses, immediately adding the remark : "And no one hath accurately
done them all, nor will you venture to say the contrary."* The quotation

---

* Dialogue with Trypho the Jew, Part ii. p. 345 of Thirlby's edition.

under the curse; for it is written, Cursed *is* every one that continueth not in all things which are written in the book of the law to do them.	γάρ· ὅτι ἐπικατάρατος πᾶς ὃς οὐκ ἐμμένει ἐν πᾶσι τοῖς γεγραμμένοις ἐν τῷ βιβλίῳ τοῦ νόμου, τοῦ

is from Deut. xxvii. 26. The Septuagint corresponds with the text here in the use of the word "continueth," ἐμμένει. The Hebrew is רָקִים, rendered in our Bible, "that confirmeth." This is the usual meaning of the word when the subject relates to keeping covenants and promises. Thus it occurs twice in Num. xxx. 15, where our translation (ver. 14) has the two words "establisheth" and "confirmeth;" and in a similar sense it is used in several of the previous verses. In 1 Sam. xv. 11 it is said of Saul, "he hath not *performed* my commandments," where the original word is the same. The meanings are closely connected, as *performing* the condition of an agreement is essential to a *confirmation* of it. The Septuagint, which St. Paul here follows, gives therefore the real meaning. Compare the quotation from Jeremiah in Heb. viii. 9, "they continued not," where the Greek both in the Old and New Testaments is the same. The Apostle here employs the language of Moses in order to express his own thought, namely, that the law denounces its curse on every individual who fails to keep it perfectly. But this is not the idea in Deuteronomy, neither is it necessary that the Hebrew legislator and the writer to the Galatians should use the words in the same meaning. Moses is speaking of particular acts of wickedness which the people are taught to regard as most abominable, and which subjected their perpetrators to a curse. So far from supposing that the laws referred to would be disregarded or but imperfectly kept, he presumes a most strict obedience. It is impossible to read the chapter without perceiving this. And that he had any deep or hidden meaning is not to be assumed.

The same principle which serves to explain this quotation is equally applicable to that in ver. 12: "The man that doeth them shall live by them." The words may be found in Levit. xviii. 5 and elsewhere, and the context shows that obedience to the precepts there enjoined is both demanded and expected of the Hebrews. But the Apostle's argument requires the words to be understood of perfect and unvarying obedience to the whole extent of God's moral law originally imposed on man. Otherwise it has no logical force. We must allow, therefore, that St. Paul does not interpret these passages of the Old Testament. He only avails himself of them to express thereby his own thoughts. In the same way he employs the language of Moses and David in Rom. x. 5–8, 18, where see the notes. This method of citing is more fully examined in the remarks on quotations in the Commentary on Hebrews, pp. 26–29, to which I refer the reader for further information.

11 ποιῆσαι αὐτά. Ὅτι δὲ ἐν νόμῳ
οὐδεὶς δικαιοῦται παρὰ τῷ Θεῷ,
δῆλον · ὅτι ὁ δίκαιος ἐκ πίστεως
12 ζήσεται · ὁ δὲ νόμος οὐκ ἔστιν
ἐκ πίστεως, ἀλλ' ὁ ποιήσας αὐτὰ
13 ζήσεται ἐν αὐτοῖς. Χριστὸς
ἡμᾶς ἐξηγόρασεν ἐκ τῆς κατάρας
τοῦ νόμου, γενόμενος ὑπὲρ ἡμῶν
κατάρα, (γέγραπται γάρ· ἐπικατ-
άρατος πᾶς ὁ κρεμάμενος ἐπὶ
14 ξύλου,) ἵνα εἰς τὰ ἔθνη ἡ εὐλο-

But that no man is justified by the 11
law in the sight of God, it is evident: for, The just shall live by
faith. And the law is not of faith; 12
but, The man that doeth them shall
live in them. Christ hath re- 13
deemed us from the curse of the
law, being made a curse for us: for
it is written, Cursed is every one
that hangeth on a tree: that the 14
blessing of Abraham might come

11. The quotation at the end of the verse is from Hab. ii. 4, and is intended as proof of the immediately preceding assertion. See its meaning
and application stated in the note on Heb. x. 38, where, and in Rom. i. 17,
it is also quoted with the same view.

12. Olshausen regards the clause, "the law is not of faith," as elliptical
for, "he who is of the law is not of faith," the institution being put for the
individual who belongs to it. But it is more emphatic to consider it as
showing the utter want of connection between law and faith. The
former has no dependence on the latter, no association with it; it ignores
it entirely. Theodoret thus: "The law does not require faith; it de-
mands works, (literally, action, conduct,) and promises life to those who
keep it."*

13. "Redeemed:" Literally, *bought off*. The idea is the same as that
elsewhere expressed by ransom, purchase, propitiation, atonement, redemption, and the expression corresponds most nearly with the first of these.—
"Made a curse:" This is the abstract for the concrete; a *curse* for an
object considered *as accursed*. We have a striking instance of the same
usage both as regards the verb and the noun in 2 Cor. v. 21: "He hath
made him to be *sin;*" that is, God *hath regarded and treated* him *as a
sinner*. That this and not sin-offering, as some say, is the meaning of the
word, is proved both from its antithesis with "righteousness" at the end
of the verse, and also from Christ's being said to "know no sin," that is,
to have been really sinless. The quotation in Galatians is from Deut.
xxi. 23, and is adduced merely to show how the condemned and capitally
punished malefactor was reputed.—"For us:" Meaning, in our place, and
for our benefit.

14. "The blessing of Abraham:" That is, the blessing promised to
him and his faithful spiritual progeny, of whom believing Gentiles are a
part, in which also Abraham participated.—"The promise of the Spirit"
does not mean, 'the blessings promised by the Spirit.' The words are

* In loc. Opera, Edit. Paris. 1642, tom. iii., p. 274.

on the Gentiles through Jesus Christ; that we might receive the promise of the Spirit through faith.

15 Brethren, I speak after the manner of men: Though *it be* but a man's covenant, yet *if it be* confirmed, no man disannulleth, or addeth

γία τοῦ 'Αβραὰμ γένηται ἐν Χριστῷ 'Ιησοῦ, ἵνα τὴν ἐπαγγελίαν τοῦ πνεύματος λάβωμεν διὰ τῆς πίστεως. 'Αδελφοί, 15 κατὰ ἄνθρωπον λέγω· ὅμως ἀνθρώπου κεκυρωμένην διαθήκην οὐδεὶς ἀθετεῖ ἢ ἐπιδιατάσ-

equivalent to 'the Spirit promised.' Ellicott prefers the phrase, "the realization of the gift of the promised Spirit," which is implied in the other. It may be the exegetical genitive, like "the sign of circumcision, the earnest of the Spirit," in Rom. iv. 11, 2 Cor. v. 5. As this communication of the Spirit was intended for Gentiles in general, it cannot be limited to his miraculous gifts.

15 et seq. The Apostle now proceeds to show that the covenant which God originally established with Abraham and his progeny cannot have been annulled by the law of Moses, as we must suppose it to have been, if observance of this law were necessary in order to secure those blessings which had been before guaranteed by this covenant. He therefore addresses himself to the understanding of his readers, and argues with them on acknowledged human analogies.

"I speak after the manner of men:" For the meaning of this phrase in the New Testament, see the note on Rom. iii. 5, p. 46. Here it does not signify, as many commentators have supposed, 'I argue weakly and in a way adapted to your imperfect comprehension;' but, 'I appeal to your understanding, as one reasonable man may properly appeal to another.' The proposition laid down as the foundation of the argument is this: that covenants entered into between man and man, after ratification, are neither lawfully annulled nor added to; they must remain unaltered. Olshausen assumes διαθήκη to mean *a testament.* He says: "St. Paul represents God's promise as a bequest, as a testament. He compares this divine testament with a human one, and infers from that comparison that the attribute of the latter, its irrevocable and unchangeable character, must surely necessarily belong to the former. What is bequeathed in the testament must be handed over to the person to whom it is bequeathed, and to no other. Thus, too, the promise of God to Abraham and his seed cannot be cancelled by the law, which was promulgated later; it remains the inalienable right of the seed of Abraham, that is, Christ." But, as a man's testament may be altered and even revoked and destroyed, the advocate of the Jewish system might have replied to such an argument, that the law was in the place of a subsequent testament revoking the former. "St. Paul," he says, "was perfectly aware that the comparison was not accurate in *all* points; he only means to speak *as a man.*" The same com-

16 σεται· τῷ δὲ ᾿Αβραὰμ ἐρρήθησαν thereto. Now to Abraham and 16

---

mentator argues in favor of the sense of testament, will, from the use of the
word "confirmed;" but this applies equally well to a covenant : "also from
the idea of an inheritance;" which, however, is to be understood in the sense
of a possession, as the land of Canaan was for the descendants of Abraham,
and as heaven is for all his spiritual progeny. The ideas of will and inheritance are, of course, often associated; but the latter does not necessarily imply the former, especially in the language of Scripture. He
refers also to Heb. ix. 16, 17; but this is unsatisfactory. See the note
there. The true meaning is "covenant" or 'dispensation' or 'arrangement,' according to its invariable usage in the Old and New Testaments.

῞Ομως· even yet. The word intimates that the representation as applied
to the divine arrangement has peculiar force. A man's covenant is indeed
sometimes infringed on; but *even yet* a comparison may be drawn from
it, as it ought not to be, and cannot legally be, annulled or altered without
the consent of the contracting parties; how much more then is this true of
a divine arrangement. Compare the use of the particle in 1 Cor. xiv. 7.
Koppe gives to ἐπιδιατάσσεται the sense of acting in opposition to. But
that of adding to is much more common; it makes a good antithesis with
"annulleth;" and is quite strong enough for the Apostle's purpose.

16. "He saith:" That is, God or the Spirit. Or, it may be understood of the Scripture, 'it saith.' Comp. Rom. xv. 10, 1 Cor. vi. 16.
The promises which God made to Abraham are sometimes made also
directly to his "seed" or progeny, as in Gen. xii. 7, xiii. 15, xv. 18, xvii. 8,
"to thy seed—to thee and to thy seed." And where this is not the case,
his spiritual progeny are also implied, inasmuch as the direct promise to
the patriarch implied the extraordinary distinction of his posterity. Thus
the declaration, "in thee shall all families of the earth be blessed," could
not possibly have been understood solely of Abraham himself, but must
have conveyed to him and to all who became acquainted with it some
reference to future progeny to be derived from him. The Apostle therefore expresses himself with most perfect accuracy when he represents the
divine promises as intended for both.

But no little difficulty has arisen from the tenor of his comment: "He
saith not, and to seeds, as of many; but as of one, and to thy seed,
which is Christ." It is supposed that, from the use of the singular number, he argues that the prophetic reference must be limited to one; whereas the original word as applied to descendants is never used in the plural,
but always in the singular.

Hence it is that Koppe maintains that the word "Christ" can only be
understood of the Lord Jesus personally. This he argues from what he
regards as the Apostle's idea, namely, that the promises so belong to

his seed were the promises made.   αἱ ἐπαγγελίαι καὶ τῷ σπέρματι

Christ, that it is in his power to make whomsoever he will partakers of them; and also from the reasoning from the singular and plural numbers. The latter argument, he says, "may seem to us to be worthless and foreign from the genius of the Hebrew language, in which the same word *seed* may signify an individual, as in Gen. iv. 25," (to which may be added xxi. 13,) "and posterity in general, as often, while on the other hand the plural form is confined to fruits, and is never used of human offspring." Still he professes to acquiesce in the interpretation of an author explaining words of his own native tongue, and especially under divine influence. What he says of the use of the Hebrew term is true, and the word *seeds*, σπέρματα, occurs in the Septuagint only six times, and always with the meaning of vegetables: See Gen. xlvii. 24, Levit. xxvi. 16, Ps. cxxv. 6, Isa. lxi. 11, Dan. i. 12, 16. In the Chaldee, indeed, the plural is employed to designate races of men: See the Targums on Gen. x. 18, Josh. vii. 14, and Jer. xxxiii. 24. Stroth also proceeds upon the same supposition with Koppe, and paraphrases thus: "But now God gave such a promise to Abraham and his progeny; where the plural term *progenies* is not used, because the discourse is not of many, but it is said expressly in the singular number, *thy progeny*, and that is Christ."

Perhaps the strongest language founded on this idea of an argument is that of Jerome, which I translate for the benefit of the English reader, giving the Latin in the note, to show that I have no intention of doing the learned father injustice. "Paul, who was made all things to all men, that he might gain all, a debtor to the Greeks and barbarians, to the wise and the unwise, to the Galatians also, whom not long before he had called fools, was made a fool. For he does not address such arguments to them as he does to the Romans, but those of the simpler sort, and which foolish persons might understand, and such as are taken from the common herd." This he thinks is intimated by the phrase, "after the manner of men," which he paraphrases thus, in the person of the Apostle himself: "For what I am about to say, I do not say according to God, nor do I say it in accordance with hidden wisdom and those who can be fed with solid food, but with them who on account of weakness of stomach are nourished with the milky dew, and are not strong enough to hear what is great."* The supposition that St. Paul adapts his argument to the silly character of the

---

* "Apostolus, qui omnibus omnia factus est, ut omnes lucrifaceret, debitor Græcis ac barbaris, sapientibus et insipientibus, Galatis quoque, quos paulo ante stultos dixerat, factus est stultus. Non enim ad eos his usus est argumentis quibus ad Romanos, sed simplicioribus, et quæ stulti possent intelligere, et pene de trivio.—Quod enim dicturus sum, non dico secundum Deum, non dico secundum reconditam sapientiam et eos qui solido possunt vesci cibo, sed secundum eos qui ob teneritudinem stomachi lacteo rore pascuntur, et nequaquam valent audire quæ grandia sunt." Comment. in Gal. Opera, Edit. Martianay, Paris. 1649, tom. iv. p. i., p. 261.

αὐτοῦ. Οὐ λέγει· καὶ τοῖς σπέρ-   He saith not, And to seeds, as of
μασιν, ὡς ἐπὶ πολλῶν, ἀλλ' ὡς   many; but as of one, And to thy

---

Galatians is wholly unfounded.   In the first place, it is by no means certain that such was their character, although this has been asserted by several writers, both ancient and modern.   The language of Themistius, as quoted by Ellicott in loc., speaks of them, on the contrary, as "quick in perception and particularly apt to learn;" and he "spent some time in the province."   And again, if the Galatians were such a stupid race as some have supposed, this would rather be a reason why they should be addressed, simply indeed, yet with arguments of sound logical force.   The laborious father founds his representation of the Apostle's mode of argument chiefly on the use of the plural *seeds*, adding, however, this important remark, which corresponds in a degree with what has already been stated, that, after revolving in his memory all the places of Scripture where the word occurs, he could not recall to mind one which was not in the singular number.

Now it is certainly worthy of consideration, whether the Apostle intends to found any argument at all on the use of the singular rather than the plural form.   I can discover no evidence that he does.   He rather seems to explain the meaning and application of the singular term, and the explanation, as will appear in the sequel, is both reasonable and scriptural. We have only to interpret the phrase "he saith," by the equivalent one, 'he means,' and the whole foundation of this supposed false or foolish argument is sapped.   And that both the Greek λέγω and the corresponding Hebrew אָמַר are so used is too clear to admit of doubt.   Indeed the very next verse to that under consideration may afford an instance, for λέγω there may as properly be rendered, 'I mean,' as, "I say."   In 1 Cor. i. 12, we have, "I say," that is, I mean "this, that each one of you," &c.; in x. 29, "conscience, I say;" that is, 'I mean.'   In John vi. 71, "he spake of (ἔλεγε, he meant) Judas Iscariot."   In Num. xxiv. 11, the Hebrew has the same meaning, and is rendered in our version, "I thought."   In 2 Sam. v. 6, the same word is translated "thinking."   So in Eccles. viii. 17: "though a wise man think (or intend) to know;" in 2 Chron. xiii. 8: "ye think," are intending; and in xxviii. 13, "ye intend."   It is therefore better to translate thus in the present instance: 'he doth not mean.'   Thus we shall have St. Paul's interpretation of the promises, and it will be to this effect, namely, that they were not intended for all the various classes of Abraham's descendants, but only for a particular one.

But it may still be asked, why does the Apostle employ the plural at all in a sense in which it never occurs in the language? why use the term "seeds" in reference to human progeny, when he must have known that usage restricted it to vegetable life? why not express his meaning by al-

17 seed, which is Christ. And this I ἐφ᾿ ἑνός· καὶ τῷ σπέρματί σου·
ὅς ἐστι Χριστός. Τοῦτο δὲ λέγω· 17

luding to some other Hebrew word, בָּנִים or יְלָדִים sons, children ? Perhaps it may be impossible satisfactorily to answer this question. But if
he chose to employ a legitimate word in the language in a different signification from its invariable one, it is evident that no misunderstanding of
his meaning could thereby arise, as this is too clearly pointed out by the
context and application of the term. And to the reader ignorant of the
Hebrew usage, as were most of the Galatians, the difficulty could not suggest itself. In 1 Cor. iv. 3, the word *day* is employed for "judgment,"
as it is translated in the English Bible ; and yet it never elsewhere has
this meaning, which, however, is clearly elicited from the context. St.
Paul could not have translated into Greek some other Hebrew word, and
based his explanation on it, for thus he would have lost sight of the original language of the promise which he meant to explain. The only difficulty lies in applying the well known plural form in a novel meaning,
which, however, the very application would suggest to the reader.

The one seed to whom the promises are represented as having been
made, is said to be Christ. But, as Drusius well remarks, he is not to
be regarded here in his individuality, but in connection with his faithful
body of which he is the head. This is certainly the Apostle's meaning,
and he is led to apply the word here in this comprehensive sense from the
revealed fact of our Lord's intimate union with his mystical body. No
other view will suit the context, especially ver. 29, "If ye be Christ's,
then are ye Abraham's seed and heirs according to the promise," which
evidently refers back to the verse before us. In Rom. iv. 13, the term
"seed" has this same general meaning, comprehending Christ and his faithful ones in union with him. See the note there, p. 67. The connection of
the head and the members is expressed in the latter clause of ver. 28, " Ye
are all one in Christ Jesus," where the masculine gender εἷς, shows that the
connection is most intimate, and that the figure is taken from an individual
person. And thus it is fully developed in Eph. iv. 13, " Until *we all* come
to *a perfect man.*" The same idea is the basis of the representation in
1 Cor. xii. 12, "As the body is one and hath many members, so also is
Christ." St. Paul's meaning, therefore, may be stated as follows : 'The
promises made to Abraham and his progeny, were not intended for all his
descendants of whatever lineage or class ; they were made to him and to
the Messiah who should spring from him, and in the latter to the patriarch's spiritual descendants also, whether of Jewish or Gentile extraction,
who should become vitally united with the Messiah by a genuine faith,
and thus be members of his mystical body.'

17. " In Christ," εἰς Χριστόν. There is considerable doubt respecting

διαθήκην προκεκυρωμένην ὑπὸ   say, *that* the covenant that was
τοῦ Θεοῦ εἰς Χριστὸν ὁ μετὰ   confirmed before of God in Christ,

---

the genuineness of these words, as they are wanting in some of the most ancient manuscripts and versions. The internal evidence may seem to be in their favor, as they agree with the view given in the previous verse; still, it cannot be denied, that on this very account they may have been originally a marginal exegetical gloss. On the supposition of their genuineness, Borger translates the preposition *until*, referring for this sense to verses 23, 24, John xiii. 1, and Acts iv. 3. This makes a very good meaning, and harmonizes with what had been before said. But the translation *to*, in the sense of *with regard to, with a view to*, is equally good. If the covenant with Abraham, or the promises made to him, were established and ratified with a direct view, also, to Christ and his faithful members, the law which was introduced subsequently, could not annul it, without a violation of the divine pledge.

"Four hundred and thirty years after:" This statement might lead to a tedious chronological disquisition, the result of which would in all probability be unsatisfactory. It would involve an examination of the question, how long the Israelites remained in Egypt. As the force of the Apostle's representation and argument does not at all depend upon the period of time which elapsed between the giving of the promise and of the law, any investigation of this point is not required in order to interpret his meaning. Still, to put the reader in possession of some information on this topic, I will mention that there are two general views, which have been maintained by their respective advocates. The one limits the time of the residence in Egypt to 215 years; the other extends it to twice that period. It may be sufficient to state a few of the prominent arguments on both sides. They may be found more fully, though still briefly, drawn out in a note in my companion to the Book of Genesis, Introduction, pp. 66, 67, and in a Dissertation by Koppe, in the Sylloge Commentationum Theologicarum, edited by Pott and Ruperti, Vol. II. pp. 255, et seq.

As Isaac was born 25 years after Abraham's removal from Haran, and as on the birth of Jacob his father was 60, and he himself 130 when he first stood before Pharaoh, it follows that the space of time between Abraham's removal to Canaan and Jacob's descent to Egypt was 215 years. This will appear by a comparison of the following texts: Gen. xii. 4, xxi. 5, xxv. 26, and xlvii. 9. The defenders of the shorter period of the sojourn in Egypt refer to the genealogy of Moses and Aaron in Exod. vi. 18, 20; to their immediate ancestry mentioned in Num. xxvi. 57, 59; and to those of Zelophehad, xxvii. 1; all of which particulars seem to coincide with their theory. They appeal also to the Septuagint and Samaritan readings of Exod. xii. 40, which contain additions to the Hebrew text, as will be seen

the law, which was four hundred and thirty years after, cannot disannul, that it should make the	τετρακόσια καὶ τριάκοντα ἔτη γεγονὼς νόμος οὐκ ἀκυροῖ, εἰς τὸ καταργῆσαι τὴν ἐπαγγελίαν.

by comparing with it the following translations. The Septuagint, as given in the Vatican manuscript, reads thus : " The sojourning of the children of Israel in the land of Egypt, and in the land of Canaan." The Alexandrine adds, " they and their fathers." The Samaritan Pentateuch agrees: "The sojourning of the children of Israel and of their fathers—in the land of Canaan and in the land of Egypt." Thus, both these authorities include within the 430 years, the 215 which elapsed from Abraham's removal from Haran to Jacob's going to Egypt.

On the other hand, in favor of a residence of 400 or 430 years, the genealogy of Joshua, in 1 Chron. vii. 20, 27, may be appealed to. There Joshua, the successor of Moses, is made to descend from Ephraim, through ten generations at least. The statements in Gen. xv. 13, and Acts vii. 6, expressly declare the residence to have been 400 years, and the phrase, " fourth generation," in Gen. xv. 16, is equivalent, as in that early period a generation might be reckoned as 100 years, both expressions being used, perhaps, as round numbers. The Hebrew of Exod. xii. 40, is also very clear in favor of the longer period. The additions of the Septuagint and Samaritan Pentateuch are evidently glosses introduced to remove a supposed chronological difficulty. They are altogether out of place. The intention of Moses is to show that the divine promises relating to the deliverance of the Hebrews were punctually verified in the fact, that, at the expiration of the period of 430 years, on the very night of its termination, God accomplished his promise and delivered them. The space of 215 years, during which their ancestors wandered about in Canaan, and indeed any reference at all to their fathers, are entirely foreign to the author's purpose. The Vatican copy of the Septuagint gives a sense bordering on the ridiculous, as it comprehends the patriarchal ancestors of the nation among the children of Israel, an absurdity which the additional clause of the Alexandrine and the Samaritan has removed.

In addition to what has been said, it may be well to note the vast increase of the Israelites during their continuance in Egypt. In Exod. xii. 37, the men are estimated at 600,000. If we add a moderately proportionate number of women and children, the aggregate can hardly be less than 2,000,000 of souls. This fact is best explained on the theory of the longer residence.

Koppe thinks that, as St. Paul's object was not to state with minute accuracy a chronological period, but only that the law was introduced but a short time comparatively after the promise to Abraham, it was indifferent to him whether the computation were made from Abraham's en-

18 Εἰ γὰρ ἐκ νόμου ἡ κληρονομία, οὐκέτι ἐξ ἐπαγγελίας· τῷ δὲ Ἀβραὰμ δι' ἐπαγγελίας κεχάρισται ὁ Θεός.

19 Τί οὖν ὁ νόμος; τῶν παρα-

promise of none effect. For if the 18 inheritance *be* of the law, *it is* no more of promise: but God gave *it* to Abraham by promise.

Wherefore then *serveth* the law? 16

---

trance into Canaan or Jacob's descent into Egypt. And Olshausen remarks that, as " the promise was given to Isaac and Jacob as well as to Abraham, St. Paul could therefore properly count from Jacob and his entry into Egypt." But this is unsatisfactory, as the promise referred to is evidently that made to the first of the patriarchs. The Apostle, no doubt, in a matter of little importance, follows the Septuagint chronology, to which his readers were accustomed.

18. That the inheritance promised to Abraham was not regarded by St. Paul as limited to the possession of Palestine is evident; for had he so understood the promise, it would have been quite gratuitous to show that it could not have been founded on a subsequently promulged law. He regards the heavenly inheritance, the blessings of Messiah's kingdom, as constituting its most prominent portion.—" Gave:" The original often expresses the idea of kindness, gratification, favor, as characterizing the gift, and therefore may well be translated, ' graciously gave.' See Luke vii. 21, Rom. viii. 32, 1 Cor. ii. 12.

19. " Wherefore, then, serveth the law?" The original is more terse and forcible: ' why then the law?' or, more in accordance with the usual meaning of τί, ' what then (is) the law?' What is its general purport, what its object?—" It was added," προσετέθη· Olshausen very judiciously remarks that the preposition is genuine, that it expresses the subsequent addition of the law, and thereby indicates its accessory character. It was something in its very nature wholly different from the spiritual covenant which God had before entered into with the patriarch.—" On account of transgressions:" No doubt the Apostle means that the law was intended to restrain transgressions, and that this was one object for which it was given. But he also refers to the office of the law in developing to the conscience the true character of sin, in rousing up against it man's fallen nature, and in making him feel his incompetency to control this nature, thus preparing him for the Gospel. See Rom. v. 20, vii. 5, 7–13, and the notes there. Olshausen says that this " mode of thinking and representation does not suit the context." But it does suit the context very well, and particularly from verse 21.

" Till the seed should come:" Christ is represented as the seed, because he is the head and source of divine life to all the spiritual progeny. And for this very reason the Apostle adds: " to whom the promise was made;" not, however, intending thereby to exclude those who belong to

4

It was added because of transgressions, till the seed should come to
whom the promise was made; *and
it was* ordained by angels in the

βάσεων χάριν προσετέθη, ἄχρις
οὗ ἔλθῃ τὸ σπέρμα, ᾧ ἐπήγγελ-
ται, διαταγεὶς δι' ἀγγέλων, ἐν

him from a claim to the same promise, by virtue of their connection with
him. The whole clause shows the transitory nature of the law, which was
to last only until the introduction of the better and fuller dispensation
by Christ.

"Ordained by angels :" Or, 'established' or 'arranged through,' that is,
by the instrumentality of 'angels.' This clause of the verse mentions the
law as established by the intervention of angels, and through Moses as
mediator. The intention seems to be, to show the dignity and excellence
of the Mosaic system, and also how perverse and wicked was the conduct
of the Israelites in neglecting and transgressing a law so gloriously introduced. This corresponds with the scope wherever the same view is given
of the introduction of the law. Thus St. Stephen, after having addressed
the Jews as "stiffnecked and uncircumcised in heart and ears, always
resisting the Holy Ghost," as "the betrayers and murderers of the just
one," adds, "who have received the law by the disposition (literally *arrangements* or *establishments*, διαταγάς, as here the Apostle uses διαταγείς,)
of angels, and have not kept it." Acts vii. 51–53. So also in Heb. ii. 2,
"If the word," or doctrine or religious system, "spoken by angels was
steadfast, and every transgression and disobedience received a just recom-
pense of reward." In the Septuagint of Deut. xxxiii. 2, the agency of
angels is mentioned in connection with the giving of the law, and these
heavenly beings seem to be intended by the words, "ten thousands of saints,"
or 'holy ones,' in the Hebrew of the same verse. Also in Ps. lxviii.
17, [18,] the author probably alludes to the multitude of angels who at-
tended the announcement of the law at Sinai. In Herod's address to his
army as given by Josephus, we find similar language, expressive of dignity. The excellent and holy law is said to have been communicated *by
angels*, δι' ἀγγέλων.* Some of the Rabbinical writers make the same
representation.—"By the hand of" is a Hebraism, בְּיַד, meaning simply
by, as in many cases it would have been better rendered in our translation,
for example in all those places where God is said to "have *spoken*" or
announced his "*word*" by the "*hand*" of Moses or any other prophet.
See Levit. x. 11, Num. iv. 45, 2 Kings xiv. 25.—Although St. Paul does
indeed represent the law as temporary, as added on account of human
sinfulness, as incompetent to annul God's previous promise with Abraham, and as merely introductory to the Gospel; yet he does not mean to

* Antiquities, Book xv. chap. v. sect. 3, Hudson's edition, p. 674.

20 χειρὶ μεσίτου. Ὁ δὲ μεσίτης hand of a mediator. Now a medi- 20

depreciate it in any of its rightful claims, and therefore notes the dignified
and glorious manner of its announcement. Still, its inferiority to the
Gospel appears even here in the fact that, while angels were the agents in
promulging the one, the Son of God descending from heaven proclaimed
the other, of which he became himself the great Mediator.

20. " Now a mediator is not of one, but God is one :" On the meaning
of this very difficult verse, which has given rise to more numerous and
diversified interpretations than any other in the Bible, I shall not pro-
nounce any definite opinion, but merely lay before the reader some of the
more prominent expositions, introducing and accompanying them with a
few remarks. It is probable that, if we had the benefit of all those oral
instructions which St. Paul had given to the Galatians when among them,
his meaning might easily be elicited, and that become luminous which is
now obscure.

The learned German writer Gfrörer,* has given a view of this text
which, so far as I know, is peculiar to himself. After saying that " its
meaning is easy to be perceived by the eye which has been sharpened by
accurate acquaintance with the Jewish mode of thought," he proceeds as
follows. ' The best interpreters rightly allow it to be the Apostle's object,
to show the inferiority of the law to the Gospel. The appointment of a
mediator grows naturally out of occasions when many are to act with
many. This was the case at the giving of the law, multitudes of angels
and the whole body of Israelites constituting the two acting parties. In
order to avoid confusion the office of internuncio or mediator is committed
to one. The mediator is not of one but of many ; on the one side, the
myriads of Israelites, and on the other, the hosts of angels. The clause,
but of many, must be added to supply the ellipsis. But God is a single
one. Hence it follows that Moses, when he received the law, was not the
mediator of God, but of angels, who required a mediator on account of their
large number. The law, therefore, is the work of angels, not of God, and
consequently far inferior to the Gospel, which springs from God and his
Son.' The author does not deny the ordinary sense of mediator as used
in Heb. viii. 6, ix. 15, xii. 24, and 1 Tim. ii. 5, for an intermediate person
between God and man. In this place, however, he gives to the word the
meaning of a substitute authorised to act in behalf of a multitude.

But however confident this learned writer may feel in an interpretation
which he supposes will be admitted by those who, like himself, are versed
in Jewish lore ; the interpretation is certainly not in harmony with scriptural analogy. Although St. Paul's intention doubtless is to show the

---

* In his History of Ancient Christianity : Geschichte des Urchristenthums, das Jahrhundert des
Heils ; Erste Abtheilung, pp. 228, 229. Stuttgart, 1838.

ator is not *a mediator* of one, but ἑνὸς οὐκ ἔστιν, ὁ δὲ ϑεὸς εἷς

---

inferiority of the law to the Gospel, as he does by the representations which he makes in the preceding and subsequent context; yet the evidence of this inferiority does not lie in the fact that the former was given by the instrumentality of angels. This is never mentioned as a depreciating circumstance. On the contrary, in the three places in which it occurs in the New Testament, it is always introduced as an honorable attestation of dignity. Compare Acts vii. 53, Heb. ii. 2, and the text under consideration, with Deut. xxxiii. 2, and Ps. lxviii. 17. Besides, it is not to be believed, without the strongest scriptural evidence, (of which there is absolutely none at all,) that the angels should have appointed Moses to act in their place, or have regarded themselves as represented by him. And, moreover, it is utterly at variance with the usual representations of Scripture, to speak of the law as emanating from angels. It was not an angelic, but a divine work; and Moses was not a mediator between angels and the Israelites, but between the Israelites and God: "I stood between the Lord (Jehovah) and you, (the Hebrews,) to show you the word of the Lord:" Deut. v. 5. With this compare Acts vii. 38: "This is he that was with the angel which spoke to him in the mount Sinai," the personage who there announced himself to be "Jehovah, the God of Abraham, of Isaac, and of Jacob," (Exod. iii. 2, 4, 6, 7,) "and with our fathers." It cannot be conceded, that the law was given by angels through Moses who acted as their agent, or as mediator between them and the Israelites. The covenant which was then made was made between them and Jehovah, the God of their patriarchal ancestors. Angels were merely the instruments of its divine author in promulging it; and their agency on the occasion contributed to its solemnity, dignity and awfulness. And, in connection with this remark, let it be noted that the language of Heb. ii. 5, "Unto the angels hath he not put in subjection the world to come whereof we speak," that is, the kingdom of the Messiah, does not justify the inference which some have drawn, namely, that the period of the Hebrew church and nation was peculiarly under angelic direction. It merely affirms that the Christian dispensation is not under angelic control, but is subjected to glorified human nature in the person of Christ.—The exposition of Gfrörer is unsupported by any scriptural warrant.

Jowett's view of the meaning is "obscure," as he himself intimates. When he says: "The Apostle is contrasting the law, which had a mediator, with the Gospel, *which was an open access to God,*" it is not easy to understand what idea he means to convey. This way of stating the contrast between the two systems would seem to imply that "the Gospel" furnished "access to God" *without a mediator.* This indeed does appear to be his meaning; for afterwards he says: "In the highest revelation of

God *there can be no mediator.*" He adds indeed the qualifying clause, " as in the Jewish religion." But if by this he merely means that Christianity has no such mediator as Judaism had, this is a mere truism. If he means that it has no mediator at all, a sense which would correspond with the previous phrase, " the Gospel was an open access to God ;" this is untrue, as is proved by the New Testament in general, and especially by the declaration in 1 Tim. ii. 5, which Jowett himself had just before quoted : " There is one mediator between God and man, the man Christ Jesus."

Conybeare states " the most natural meaning to be as follows : It is better to depend upon an unconditional promise of God than upon a covenant made between God and man. For in the latter case the conditions of the covenant might be broken by man, (as they had been,) and so the blessings forfeited ; whereas in the former case, God being immutable, the blessings derived from his promise remain steadfast forever." But this depends upon the supposition that God's promises, as revealed in Scripture, are " unconditional" and absolute; and this is the very point which cannot be admitted, simply because it cannot be proved.

Barnes, in his notes on this passage, expresses the opinion that the term " mediator" is here intended not of Moses but of Christ, to whom " the name is always applied in the New Testament." He thinks that by stating the law to have been introduced by him as Mediator, the Apostle shows that it " was subordinate to the Messiah and with reference to him ;" and that " angels must themselves be inferior to him, the mediator between God and man." He presumes the meaning of the first clause to be, " that a mediator always supposes two parties ;" and of the second, " that God is the same one God in whatever form his will may be made known to man, whether by a promise—as to Abraham, or by the law—as to Moses." The same want of close connection between the two clauses which has been already noted is here also apparent. And although the very word " mediator" is not indeed directly applied elsewhere to Moses, yet his whole history from the period of the Exode until his death is one continued development of this character. Moreover his action as such between the Jehovah-angel and the church is asserted by St. Stephen in Acts vii. 38, and " between the Lord and Israel" by Moses himself in Deut. v. 5. Besides, the word only occurs, exclusive of this place, four times in the Bible, and always in reference to Christ as mediator of the Gospel, " the new and better covenant." See 1 Tim. ii. 5, Heb. viii. 6, ix. 15, xii. 24. He is never spoken of as mediator between God and the Hebrews, mediator of the law.

A very natural sense of the first clause, and which is given by several commentators is this : ' A mediator of one is not ;' that is, to call a person a mediator whose intercourse is confined to one party is a contradiction,

two parties being essential to the idea of mediator. Thus the clause simply expresses the necessary condition of mediatorial action. What then is
the meaning of the latter clause? and how is it connected with the preceding? It may be said that this merely expresses the idea of the un-
changeableness of God, who therefore would not by the law annul the previous promise to Abraham. But this is not satisfactory. St. Paul is a
close writer, and some close connection seems evidently to have been intended between—" a mediator *of one*," and—" God is *one*."

Locke gives the same general view of the former clause, and explains
the latter so as to make a very close connection. He remarks that St.
Paul " is proving that the law could not disannul the promise or covenant,"
because, " once ratified, it cannot be altered or disannulled by any other
than both the parties concerned. God is but one of the parties concerned
in the promise; the Gentiles and Israelites together make up the other:
ver. 14. But Moses, at the giving of the law, was a mediator only between
the Israelites and God, and therefore could not transact anything to the
disannulling the promise, which was between God and the Israelites together, because God was but one of the parties to that covenant; the other,
which was the Gentiles as well as Israelites, Moses appeared or transacted
not for." But, it may be replied, if the covenant, or rather the promise, were
made to Abraham and his spiritual progeny, all of the latter then living
of whom anything is known were congregated at Mount Sinai, and the two
parties were as much present as they then could be. And if the presence
of the Gentile portion and of the whole body were necessary, it may be
said that such an attendance never could take place, as the party consisted
of successive generations of Israelites and Gentiles, and extended to all
subsequent ages. To me, however, the great objection to this view lies
here: that it represents God's covenant with Abraham too much in the
light of a merely human agreement, thus putting God and man in the
transaction upon an equality. True, the divine arrangement made with
the patriarch was in a certain sense a covenant, in which God pledged himself to grant certain benefits. But that the formal consent of the human
party must have been obtained in order to effect an alteration of this
arrangement, is not to be conceded. What is usually called a covenant
in our Bibles is, properly speaking, a disposition or arrangement on the
part of God; and whether it be revocable or not depends not upon man's
consent but upon God's will and purpose.

Olshausen takes the same view of the first clause: " The idea is that
of every mediator as such; *not of one* shows that a mediator necessarily
presupposes *two; one* cannot be represented by a mediator." On the
latter clause he remarks as follows: " We may translate, *God is one* or *a
single one.*" Hence he infers that he also is " consequently only one
party." St. Paul " meant (ver. 19) to set forth the relative excellence

of the law, but in such a way that its inferiority to the Gospel should also be ever apparent. Mediation presumes separation; one cannot be mediated for. Since God is the *one* part, there must also have been *a second*, mankind, who were separated from God." He then proceeds to say that Christ, having united all to God and separation no longer existing, "all mediators appear superfluous." He does not deny the mediatorial character of Christ; on the contrary, he refers to 1 Tim. ii. 5, and Eph. ii. 14, in support of the doctrine. Only he supposes that here the Apostle views the mediatorial work as accomplished on account of the union of God and man in Christ, which union, "he communicates by degrees to the faithful." He has not applied the words of the text so as to develop his view with sufficient clearness. But this much is evident, that it presumes a regard to the Christian scheme as completely finished, and the whole body of the faithful as having come to their ultimate perfection of divine union; until which consummation a mediator is not superfluous, but essential. But this method of viewing the two dispensations is unfair, as it compares the *initiation* of the law with the *consummation* of the Gospel. Still, St. Paul may intend to set mediator and God in contradistinction to each other, the former as the agent of the law, and the latter as the author of the promise. The superior excellence of the promise would be shown in this respect, that mediation implies separation of the parties between whom it takes place, and such was the condition of God and the Hebrews at the promulgation of the law. However, it cannot be denied that such also is the condition of mankind in general in reference to their Maker until the reception of the Gospel.

Borger and Koppe agree in the general view. They both understand *law* after *of one*, and the former introduces the particle *indeed*, explaining the clause thus: "established indeed by angels through a mediator, but a mediator is not of this one law; the Christian system also has its own mediator, Christ Jesus." Thus the Apostle is made to imply that the mediatorial function is not limited to the law of Moses, appealing to what the Galatians well knew to be the truth. Koppe differs slightly. He does not restrict the comparison to Christ and Moses, but paraphrases thus: "It is not the law of Moses only that has its own mediator, (there were more and especially Jesus the mediator of the new covenant,) but God is one and the same, who sent them all; he therefore ought to be and must be consistent with himself." To illustrate the use of *law* or *system* in connection with *mediator*, he appeals to Heb. viii. 6, ix. 15, where the full expression, "mediator of a better, of the new covenant," occurs. In reply to the objection that this view loses sight of the intimate connection between *of one* and *one*, Borger remarks that St. Paul frequently uses the same word even in opposite senses in the same construction, as in Romans viii. 2, "the *law of the Spirit of life* hath made me free from the *law of sin and death*," and in other places.   This is true; but it does not remove the difficulty, as here the close connection of the general thought seems to require a similar signification in the words.   Besides, it is a serious objection to this view that it obliges us to supply the most prominent idea, namely, that the new covenant has its mediator as well as the old.

For the satisfaction of the reader, I transcribe the latter half of Ellicott's note.   "The context is a brief but perspicuous statement of the four distinctive features of the law, (see above,) with tacit reference to the promise.   Three of these are passed over; the last, as the most important, is noticed: 'the law was with, the promise was without a mediator.'   Verse 20 thus appears a syllogism of which the conclusion is omitted: '*Now every mediator appertains not to one* (but two).   *But* (in the promise) *God is one* (not two).   (Therefore in the promise a mediator appertains not to God.)   *Is then the law* (a dispensation which, besides other distinctions, involved a mediator,) *opposed to the promises which rested* (alone) *on God* (and involved no mediator)?   *No, verily.*   The only difficulty is in the prop. minor.   *How* was God one, not two?"   After giving Baur's "manifestly insufficient" answer, he proceeds: "God was one, because he was both giver and receiver united; giver as the Father, receiver as the Son, the seed to whom the promise was made.   Thus everything becomes forcible, logical, and, as the very brevity would lead us to expect, theologically significant and profound."

Omitting some serious objections to this representation, I conclude this already too much extended note by introducing one other view of which the verse is susceptible.

The interpretations just given presume the word "mediator" with the article to be comprehensive, and expressive of the character in general.   This is certainly not only allowable, but quite natural; and the article is often employed in this way.   Thus, in John ii. 25, it is applied twice where the Evangelist means *man* in the sense of human nature; and in iv. 1 of this very Epistle it designates character, δ $\kappa\lambda\eta\rho o\nu\delta\mu o\varsigma$ being equivalent to *any* or *every heir*.   But, on the other hand, it is also often and most commonly used to mark what is definite, and sometimes to denote distinction.   For example, in John xi. 28, we have, "*The* master is come," and in xiii. 13, "Ye call me *the* master and *the* Lord."   It may have the same distinctive force in this place.   The intention of the Apostle in the whole verse may be to introduce what is the great characteristic of the Gospel, namely, that the illustrious mediator thereof is not the mediator of one race or class or body of men, as Moses was, but of all mankind, adding what is closely connected with this thought, that God is one and the same, equally the father of all.   Comp. Rom. iii. 29, 'Since God is one who will justify both Jews and Gentiles by the same faith.'   The intro-

21 ἐστιν. Ὁ οὖν νόμος κατὰ τῶν
ἐπαγγελιῶν τοῦ Θεοῦ; μὴ γέν-
οιτο· εἰ γὰρ ἐδόθη νόμος ὁ
δυνάμενος ζωοποιῆσαι, ὄντως
ἂν ἐκ νόμου ἦν ἡ δικαιοσύνη·
22 ἀλλὰ συνέκλεισεν ἡ γραφὴ τὰ
πάντα ὑπὸ ἁμαρτίαν, ἵνα ἡ
ἐπαγγελία ἐκ πίστεως Ἰησοῦ
Χριστοῦ δοθῇ τοῖς πιστεύουσι.
23 Πρὸ τοῦ δὲ ἐλθεῖν τὴν πίστιν

God is one. *Is* the law then 21
against the promises of God? God
forbid: for if there had been a law
given which could have given life,
verily righteousness should have
been by the law. But the Scrip- 22
ture hath concluded all under sin,
that the promise by faith of Jesus
Christ might be given to them that
believe. But before faith came, 23

---

duction of these two remarks is quite natural, especially to a mind filled
with ideas of the supreme excellence of the Gospel.

21, 22. St. Paul now resumes his logical train of thought. Since the
law cannot annul the previous promise; since the heavenly inheritance is
not obtained from it; since it is a dispensation introduced indeed with
dignity and glory, but still temporary and introductory to that of the
Gospel; since, in a word, it has nothing in common with the Gospel; "is
it against the promises of God?" Is there any opposition, any contrariety
between the two? This he denies in his usual emphatic manner. But his
language is elliptical, and the ellipsis may easily be supplied by what he
had before said. The law, although not hostile to God's gracious promise
and covenant made with Abraham in reference to Christ, is nevertheless
incompetent to meet the requisitions of the fallen state of human nature.
If a law were given which could have imparted life, justification would
certainly have come from such a law. But as no law or system of law
can do this, the Scripture regards all mankind as shut up, confined in a
prison, as it were, under the dominion of sin, in order that the blessing of
the promise which flows solely from faith in Christ might be given to believers. The shutting up all under sin here ascribed to the Scripture, as
is also the foreseeing in ver. 8, is, in the parallel place, Rom. xi. 32, at-
tributed to God. The phrase is explained in the note there, p. 210.—The
reader will observe that the neuter τὰ πάντα, which the author elsewhere
uses of intelligent beings, (see Eph. i. 10 and Col. i. 20,) is immediately
followed by the masculine, "those who believe." Similar cases occur
elsewhere. Thus in John i. 11, "he came unto his own, (neuter,) but his
own (masculine,) received him not;" vi. 37, "*All that* (neut.,) the Father
giveth me will come to me, and *him that cometh*," (mas.;) xvii. 2, "*all that*
(neut. sing.,) thou hast given him, he should give *to them*," (mas. plur.;)
1 John v. 4, 5, "*whatsoever is born* (neut.,) of God overcometh the world:
who is *he that overcometh?*" (mas.)

23–25. "Schoolmaster," παιδαγωγός· This word was employed by
the ancients to designate the slave or inferior domestic attendant, who

we were kept under the law, shut	ὑπὸ νόμον ἐφρουρούμεθα συγκε-
up unto the faith which should	κλεισμένοι εἰς τὴν μέλλουσαν
24 afterwards be revealed. Where-	πίστιν ἀποκαλυφθῆναι. Ὥστε 24
fore the law was our schoolmaster	ὁ νόμος παιδαγωγὸς ἡμῶν γέγον-
to bring us unto Christ, that we	εν εἰς Χριστόν, ἵνα ἐκ πίστεως
25 might be justified by faith. But	δικαιωθῶμεν· ἐλθούσης δὲ τῆς 25
after that faith is come, we are no	πίστεως οὐκέτι ὑπὸ παιδαγωγόν

trained his master's children and conducted them to the public schools, giving them also some slight instruction himself. It means an 'instructor', but conveys also the idea of παιδεία, discipline, and even of harshness. In 1 Cor. iv. 15 it is employed in contradistinction to parental tenderness: "Though ye have ten thousand *instructors*, παιδαγωγούς, in Christ, yet have ye not many *fathers :* for in Christ Jesus I have begotten you." It is true, as Ellicott remarks, that "there is some difficulty in finding a suitable translation : 'boy's conductor,' (Peile,) is too bald,'and even insufficient; 'schoolmaster,' introduces an idea not in the original; 'pedagogue,' (Rheims Text,) is open to the same objection, though in a less degree, from having become partially obsolete. 'Tutor,' though not an unsuitable translation, here tends to obscure the idea of *custodia*, which seems the prevailing one of the passage. We therefore fall back on 'pedagogue,' as the least objectionable. This pedagogic function of the law was displayed *positively* in warnings and threatenings; *negatively*, (the prevailing idea,) in awakening the conscience and bringing a conviction of sin."

Faith here, as occasionally elsewhere, has an objective meaning. It signifies the gospel as a system of faith. Thus the statement will be that, during the continuance of the law, men were kept guarded and confined, as it were, until, or for, that is, with a view to, the revelation of the Gospel. The law is represented as a disciplinary institution preparatory to this revelation of justification by faith, on the establishment of which, men are no longer subjected to such a course of discipline. But, although faith is certainly used here in the objective meaning, yet it may comprehend also its more usual subjective signification, namely, the principle of faith in the mind of the believer. The language of St. Paul may well be regarded as describing the internal condition of the man. Before the coming of faith, as an element entering into his religious nature, he is a prisoner under law waiting for release. The law exercises a harsh discipline over him, and thus prepares him for the reception of a justifying faith. And when this faith becomes an inmate of his breast, the legal discipline ceases. He is justified and at peace with God. All this is true of a man, whether he be living under the Mosaic or Christian dispensation. See the fifth remark, appended to the commentary on Rom. vii., p. 123. With the phrases in vs. 23, 25, "before faith came, after that faith is come,"

26 ἐσμεν. Πάντες γὰρ υἱοὶ Θεοῦ
ἐστε διὰ τῆς πίστεως ἐν Χριστῷ
27 Ἰησοῦ· ὅσοι γὰρ εἰς Χριστὸν
ἐβαπτίσθητε, Χριστὸν ἐνεδύσα-
28 σθε. Οὐκ ἔνι Ἰουδαῖος οὐδὲ
Ἕλλην, οὐκ ἔνι δοῦλος οὐδὲ

longer under a schoolmaster. For 26
ye are all the children of God by
faith in Christ Jesus. For as many 27
of you as have been baptized into
Christ have put on Christ. There 28
is neither Jew nor Greek, there is

---

compare the similar language, " when the commandment came," in Rom.
vii. 9, which is used of the efficacy of the law on the awakening conscience. See the note there, p. 112.

26, 27. " For," in each of these verses, has an illative force. In the
former, the connection is this : ' You are no longer subject to the preparatory disciplinarian, and in a condition like that of a servant, for by faith in
Christ you have been placed in a state of adoption and sonship.' This implies a state of liberty, and as such it is contrasted with that of a servant.
See iv. 1, 3, 5, where those who were in bondage are said to be redeemed
and made sons. In the latter verse it may be stated thus : ' You are sons
of God, for having been baptized into Christ, you have thereby, not only
assumed a profession of his faith and character, but have become incorporated with his mystical body.' The Apostle, of course, has in view the in-
itiatory sacrament of Christianity as it is defined in 1 Pet. iii. 21 to be, " not
the putting away of the filth of the flesh, but the answer of a good conscience towards God." Such a baptism is both external and internal, both
a change of outward relation toward God's church, and a change of inward
nature. See the note on Rom. vi. 3, pp. 97, 98. To put on Christ implies a participation in the character of Christ and a union with him.
The figure denotes a possession of the reality of what it describes. For
the true scriptural sense of it, see the note just referred to, and compare
the language in 1 Cor. xv. 53, 54, where the corruptible and mortal body is
described as " putting on incorruption and immortality" at the general
resurrection. The remark of Chrysostom is exceedingly pertinent :
" Thus we say, with regard to friends, such a one has put on such a one,
when we mean to describe great love and unceasing harmony and union.
For he who has clothed himself appears to be that with which he is
clothed. Let Christ, therefore, always appear in us. And how shall he
appear ? If you do the things which are his ; that is, obey his commands."*
Ὅσοι is not accurately translated by " as many of you ;" and Conybeare's version, " whosoever among you," is equally erroneous. It means,
' ye whosoever.'

St. Paul does not mean that all outward distinctions of condition, of
inferiority and subjection or the contrary, should cease under the Chris-

---

* Hom. in Ep. ad Rom. xxiv. sect. 4. Opera, tom. ix. p. 699.

neither bond nor free, there is ἐλεύθερος, οὐκ ἔνι ἄρσεν καὶ
neither male nor female: for ye θῆλυ· πάντες γὰρ ὑμεῖς εἰς ἐστε
29 are all one in Christ Jesus. And ἐν Χριστῷ Ἰησοῦ. Εἰ δὲ ὑμεῖς 29
if ye *be* Christ's, then are ye Abra- Χριστοῦ, ἄρα τοῦ Ἀβραὰμ σπέρ-
ham's seed, and heirs according μα ἐστέ, καὶ κατ᾽ ἐπαγγελίαν
to the promise.   κληρονόμοι.

tian scheme; for this would be contradictory to what he often says elsewhere. His remarks are confined to the religious advantages of this mystical union with Christ. In these respects all are on an equality. The masculine εἷς denotes the closeness of the union. Some manuscripts read the
neuter, a very unwarrantable change of the text. See the note on ver. 16,
p. 46.

29. Δέ is best rendered *but*. It is adversative of what has been before said. But if ye have put on Christ, &c., ver. 27. To be Christ's
is to belong to him, to be members of his spiritual body ; thus the phrase
occurs in v. 24, " they that are Christ's have crucified the flesh ;" also, in
1 Cor. xv. 23, " afterward they that are Christ's." This is the condition
of being Abraham's spiritual progeny, and partakers of the same spiritual benefits which the patriarch enjoyed.

SECTION III.

Chap. IV. 1-20.

THE LEGAL AND CHRISTIAN CONDITIONS ILLUSTRATED. THE APOSTLE EX-
PRESSES HIS DEEP FEELING AT THE DEFECTION OF THE GALATIANS FROM
THEIR FORMER STATE OF CHRISTIAN CHARACTER.

IV. Now I say, *that* the heir, as long Λέγω δέ, ἐφ᾽ ὅσον χρόνον ὁ IV.
as he is a child, differeth nothing κληρονόμος νήπιός ἐστιν, οὐδὲν
from a servant, though he be lord διαφέρει δούλου, κύριος πάντων
2 of all; but is under tutors and ὤν, ἀλλὰ ὑπὸ ἐπιτρόπους ἐστὶ 2
governors until the time appointed καὶ οἰκονόμους ἄχρι τῆς προθεσ-

iv. 1, 2. St. Paul now draws a parallel between the state of a minor subjected to persons appointed to teach and control him until he arrives at an age
to be his own master, and that of man anterior to his reception of the Gospel.
It is not improbable that he has in mind the Roman usage of subjecting
boys to domestic instruction and discipline, until the time of their assum-
ing the toga virilis and being regarded as Roman citizens. Antiquarians
differ respecting the age at which this ceremony took place, some fixing it

3 μίας τοῦ πατρός. Οὕτω καὶ ἡμεῖς, ὅτε ἦμεν νήπιοι, ὑπὸ τὰ στοιχεῖα τοῦ κόσμου ἦμεν δεδου-
4 λωμένοι· ὅτε δὲ ἦλθε τὸ πλή-ρωμα τοῦ χρόνου, ἐξαπέστειλεν ὁ Θεὸς τὸν υἱὸν αὑτοῦ, γενόμε-νον ἐκ γυναικός, γενόμενον ὑπὸ

of the father. Even so we, when 3 we were children, were in bondage under the elements of the world: but when the fulness of the time 4 was come, God sent forth his Son, made of a woman, made under the

---

at the end of the 15th and others of the 16th year. Others again, suppose the period to have varied according to paternal direction,* and that this is alluded to in the phrase, "the time appointed by the father." It seems probable, however, that the age at which so important a ceremony should take place would be fixed either by law or usage. In the expression, "tutors and governors," some expositors make a distinction, considering the former term as denoting a guardian supplying the place of the deceased or absent parent, and the latter as the steward to whom the management of the estate was entrusted. Others, however, regard the distinction as arbi-trary, inasmuch as the two words are often used by Greek writers as con-vertible terms. The heir, while in his minority, is said " to differ nothing from a servant, though he be lord of all." The meaning is, that although prospectively he is the master of the paternal estate, yet as regards his condition of subjection and discipline, he is on the same footing as the servant.

3. " When we were children :" That is, before the coming of the Gos-pel and our reception of it.—Although the Apostle undoubtedly has the Jewish converts chiefly in mind, (comp. iii. 24, 25,) yet the remark ap-plies to all who were living under the influence of a merely external, and consequently, imperfect religious system. " Elements" or " rudiments of the world :" This clause denotes an elementary and imperfect religion, consisting chiefly of outward rites, and adapted to a gross and worldly condition of mind. The application of the epithet, "worldly," does not prove these elementary institutions, arrangements and services to be at all sinful ; imperfection and adaptation to a very imperfect moral and reli-gious condition are the ideas intended to be conveyed. Thus in vs. 9, 10, they are called weak and poor elements, such as Jewish ordinances and observances. In Col. ii. 8, 20, the same language occurs, and with the same meaning. And in Heb. ix. 1, the Mosaic sanctuary is called a worldly one, in the same sense of imperfection, and, as such, is contrasted with the heavenly sanctuary above. See the note there, p. 113, and com-pare viii. 5, ix. 11, 23.

4. " The fulness of the time :" To this corresponds " the time ap-

---

* See Anthon's Roman Antiquities, chap. xxvii. sect. xix. p. 284.

5 law, to redeem them that were
under the law, that we might re-
6 ceive the adoption of sons. And
because ye are sons, God hath sent
forth the Spirit of his Son into
your hearts, crying, Abba, Father.

νόμον, ἵνα τοὺς ὑπὸ νόμον ἐξα- 5
γοράσῃ, ἵνα τὴν υἱοθεσίαν ἀπο-
λάβωμεν. Ὅτι δέ ἐστε υἱοί, 6
ἐξαπέστειλεν ὁ Θεὸς τὸ πνεῦμα
τοῦ υἱοῦ αὐτοῦ εἰς τὰς καρδίας
ὑμῶν, κρᾶζον· ἀββᾶ ὁ πατήρ.

pointed by the father," in the illustration before introduced. It means, when the proper time determined by God had arrived. This period was no doubt fixed upon by divine wisdom with a foreknowledge and regard to the condition of mankind for receiving the Gospel then to be introduced. "Made:" In both instances, *born* would be preferable. The first clause merely denotes our Lord's humanity, like the same phrase in Job xiv. 1, and Matt. xi. 11, without any reference to his miraculous conception; the second, his religious relations as a Jew, subject to the Mosaic law.

5. "To redeem": Literally, buy off, as in iii. 13. The Apostle applies his remarks to Jews who "were born under the law;" not intending, of course, to limit the redemption to these, but because the scope of his discourse required such a specification. Sonship is the natural consequence of this liberation.

6. A consequent of sonship is such a communication of the Spirit as enables the recipient to regard God as a reconciled father. Borger objects to the translation, "because ye are sons God hath sent forth the Spirit." He introduces an ellipsis which, he says, is usual also in Demosthenes, and translates ὅτι *that*, giving the meaning as follows: "But, to make it evident that ye are sons, God, I say, hath sent his Spirit into your hearts." He argues that sonship does not precede the giving of the Spirit, but on the contrary is thereby produced, appealing to Rom. viii. 14, 15, where the Christian's recognition of God as his father is stated to be the result of a previous reception of the Spirit, and remarking that, according to the usual interpretation, the next verse is feeble. Hammond takes the same view: "That you are sons appears by this, that God hath sent his Spirit into your hearts," &c. So also Ellicott: "And *as a proof* that ye ARE sons, God hath," &c. Borger's charge of feebleness is mere unsupported opinion; and to his argument it is sufficient to reply that, although the Holy Spirit does indeed, by regenerating the man, produce the state of filiation, yet more abundant and subsequent communications of his influence may well be understood, whereby the child of God recognises with joyous affection his spiritual relationship. That this influence cannot be restricted to mere gifts is plain from its being spoken of as imparted to all the children of God and to their hearts, as appears also from Rom. v. 5. In the parallel place Rom. viii. 15, the act of crying father is ascribed to the Christian; here it is predicated of the spirit. The difference of phrase-

7 ʺΩστε οὐκέτι εἶ δοῦλος, ἀλλ᾽
  υἱός· εἰ δὲ υἱός, καὶ κληρονόμος
8 Θεοῦ διὰ Χριστοῦ. ᾿Αλλὰ τότε
  μὲν οὐκ εἰδότες Θεὸν ἐδουλεύ-
  σατε τοῖς φύσει μὴ οὖσι θεοῖς·
9 νῦν δὲ γνόντες Θεόν, μᾶλλον δὲ

Wherefore thou art no more a ser- 7
vant, but a son; and if a son, then
an heir of God through Christ.
Howbeit then, when ye knew not 8
God, ye did service unto them
which by nature are no gods. But 9

ology, and also the association of both the Chaldee and Greek words, are
explained in the note on that passage, p. 133.—" The Spirit of his Son :"
That is, the same Holy Spirit who descended on Christ at his baptism, who
was given to him without measure, by whom he wrought miracles. True
Christians have the same Spirit that operated in Christ, and who is therefore said to be his. But the inference which Koppe draws from this truth,
namely, that " the Spirit of his Son" is not the Spirit as sent by Christ, is
unwarrantable. Although the Holy Spirit, who was so fully given to
Christ, may well be called his on this account, yet another and much more
important reason for the expression is this, that the Son sent him to his
Apostles and to all the faithful.—It ought to be noted, that the same expression, " hath sent forth," is employed both here and in ver. 4 of the
mission of Christ and of the Spirit, and that both equally imply personality
in the one sent.

7. Here the Christian state of liberty, filiation, and heirship, is contrasted with the legal one of servitude and degradation.—Compare our
Lord's language in John viii. 32, 34, 35, where sonship and servitude to
sin are similarly contrasted. Several critics regard the words, " of God
through Christ," as an addition to the original text. They are wanting in
some of the earliest manuscripts and versions. In their place a great
variety of readings has been substituted, such as, *of God* simply, *on account of God, of God Christ, through Christ, through Jesus Christ,* &c.,
all of which, with the reading in the received text, also, Olshausen regards as glosses added to the originally concluding word " heir," which
seemed to the transcribers to make the termination too abrupt. If the
received words be genuine, as the internal evidence seems to indicate, the
words *son* and *heir* must each be connected with the word *God.*

8-11. St. Paul now endeavors to show the Galatians the inconsistency
and absurdity of relapsing into a religious system chiefly external, by re-
minding them of their former idolatrous condition, and of the divine favor
which they had experienced in their conversion to Christianity. Hence it
appears that at least a large proportion of them were of Gentile extraction,
as the idolatry here affirmed of them would not apply to the Jews. Although the verb *to serve, δουλεύειν,* is often used to express the true filial
worship of God, as in 1 Chron. xxviii. 9, " serve him with a perfect heart,"
Matt. vi. 24, " ye cannot serve God and mammon;" yet the connection in

now, after that ye have known God, or rather are known of God, how turn ye again to the weak and beggarly elements, whereunto ye 10 desire again to be in bondage? ye observe days, and months, and 11 times, and years. I am afraid of you, lest I have bestowed upon you

γνωσθέντες ὑπὸ Θεοῦ, πῶς ἐπιστρέφετε πάλιν ἐπὶ τὰ ἀσθενῆ καὶ πτωχὰ στοιχεῖα, οἷς πάλιν ἄνωθεν δουλεύειν θέλετε; Ἡμέρας παρατηρεῖσθε 10 καὶ μῆνας καὶ καιροὺς καὶ ἐνιαυτούς· Φοβοῦμαι ὑμᾶς, μη- 11 πως εἰκῆ κεκοπίακα εἰς ὑμᾶς.

which it here stands seems to imply slavish and degraded subjugation. Thus it corresponds with the language of the next verse, which expresses servile subjection to the law.

It has been supposed that Jewish converts must be meant, because they are represented as *returning* to the weak and poor, that is, jejune and empty, elementary and external religion, which is immediately described as the superstitious observance of Jewish institutions. But this difficulty will not sanction a forced exposition of the 8th verse. It is probable, therefore, that the Apostle classes all merely outward systems of religion within the same category, and considers a dependence on Jewish rites as substantially equivalent to a return to the externals of Heathenism, in the language of Koppe, to "a similar burden of useless rites." It is suggested by Olshausen, that these original Gentile idolaters may have been before their conversion Jewish proselytes, either of righteousness or of the gate. But the Epistle does not contain an intimation of this kind, neither is' the supposition at all probable.

"But now, having known God, or rather having been known by God:" The first participle merely expresses in general such a knowledge of God as conversion implies. The second amplifies the thought, and makes God the agent and the Galatians recipients of his bounty. Some commentators, following the usage of the Hebrew Hophal, explain it thus: 'having been made to know, taught, by God.' But no doubt it conveys the idea of affection, as the verb is used in Amos iii. 2: "You only have I *known*," and John x. 14: "I *know* my sheep and am *known* of mine;" 1 Cor. viii. 3: "if any man love God, the same is *known* of him;" 2 Tim. ii. 19: "the Lord *knoweth* them that are his." The words of the text are therefore best translated thus: 'having been kindly regarded by God.'—"Weak and poor:" Compare Heb. vii. 18, where "the weakness and unprofitableness" of the law are spoken of.

Πάλιν ἄνωθεν· This expression may be pleonastic for πάλιν simply, as the two words occur in the Wisdom of Solomon, xix. 6, and are translated in the authorised version "anew." Similar redundant expressions occur elsewhere, as in John xxi. 16 and Acts x. 15, where "the second time" is added to the adverb "again." Or, it may be, as Ellicott says, that

12 Γίνεσθε ὡς ἐγώ, ὅτι κἀγὼ ὡς ὑμεῖς, ἀδελφοί, δέομαι ὑμῶν· labor in vain. Brethren, I be- 12 seech you, be as I *am*; for I *am* as ye *are*; ye have not injured me at

---

" there is no pleonasm in" the phrase. It may convey " two ideas, *relapse to* bondage and *recommencement of* its principles ;" and the accurate translation may be, *again anew*, or, *even again*. In either case, the general sense will not be affected.—"Ye observe," παρατηρεῖσθε· The verb implies great care and attention. It may be chosen to intimate a superstitious scrupulosity; although this supposition is rather a result of the circumstances of the case than a meaning of the word determined by usage. The observances referred to are plainly Jewish. "Years" relates, no doubt, to the Sabbatical and Jubilee years.—"I am afraid of you;" Ὑμᾶς may be governed by κατά understood, and the meaning be, 'I am apprehensive with regard to you, lest,' &c.

12. The brevity of expression in this verse makes it exceedingly difficult to perceive the thought. Some suppose an ellipsis of ἐγενόμην or ἤμην after κἀγώ, and regard it as an exhortation to imitate the Apostle's example in abandoning undue attachment to the Mosaic ritual, thus: 'be as I am,' disenthralled from the trammels of the law; to arrive at such a condition is quite practicable, 'for I also (was once) as you (now are,)' bound down by this burdensome yoke. If St. Paul could rise superior to the control of education and association, they also could throw off a burden which they had but lately assumed. This interpretation seems to have been adopted by Justin Martyr, who addresses the Greeks thus: "Be as I, for I was as you," introducing in the latter clause the word ἤμην.*

Another view regards the words as the language of affection and intimate union; as if the author had said, ' be ye (towards me) as if ye were I, for I am (towards you) as if I were you.' Association in purpose and harmonious action in war are expressed in terms somewhat similar in 2 Chron. xviii. 3, where Jehoshaphat proffers his assistance to Ahab in the the words, "I am as thou art, and my people as thy people." This meaning agrees with the deeply affectionate language of the context, " brethren, I beseech you ;" and also with the concluding clause, "ye have not injured me at all," which shows that St. Paul was willing to overlook and forget the calumnies of his Galatian opponents, and the injuries they had attempted to inflict upon him. The other meaning loses sight of the close connection between the former and latter clauses of the verse.

Ellicott denies that such a close connection is allowable. I transcribe his note for the consideration of the critical reader, merely remarking that the natural flow of thought seems to sanction the connection objected to,

---

* Ad Græcos Oratio, sect. 5, Opera, Edit. Cong. S. Mauri, Paris. 1742, p. 5.

5

13 all. Ye know how through in-   οὐδέν με ἠδικήσατε· οἴδατε δέ, 13
  firmity of the flesh I preached the   ὅτι δι᾿ ἀσθένειαν τῆς σαρκὸς
14 gospel unto you at the first: and   εὐηγγελισάμην ὑμῖν τὸ πρότε-

and to be opposed to the supposition that the Apostle, in the words, οὐδέν
με ἠδικήσατε, alludes to any "trying circumstances" of his "first visit:"
If these words were intended to bear upon the state of feeling among the
Galatians at the time of that visit, it would seem more natural to have introduced them in direct antithesis to the statement in ver. 14, and consequently after οἴδατε, &c. However, we ought not to decide upon an
author's meaning, solely on the ground that a certain construction seems
to us most reasonable.—" Ye injured me in nothing. There is some difficulty in the connection. The majority of commentators find in these
words a declaration ὅτι οὐ μίσους οὐδὲ ἔχθρας ἦν τὰ εἰρημένα, Chrys.; the
sentiment being, 'there is nothing personal between us;' 'quod vos durius
increpavi, non feci contumeliose, tanquam injuria lacessitus,' Est. (Pol. Syn.)
This implies a connection with the preceding rather than the succeeding
words, which both the aorist (not pres. or perf.) and the adversative clause
οἴδατε δὲ (scitis potius) seem clearly to negative. It thus appears most
correct to replace (with Tisch.) the usual colon after ὑμῶν by a period, to
connect οὐδ. με ἠδ. with ver. 13 and 14 (which really do form a single
period), and to refer the aorist to St. Paul's first visit to the Galatians;
the sentiment then is, 'when I first came among you, and that under trying circumstances to you, far from wronging me, ye received me as an
angel of God.' The former affection of the Galatians is used by the Apostle
as a reason why they should now accede to his entreaties."

13, 14. The author now gladly turns the attention of the Galatians to
their former state of affection for him, describing it in very strong and
figurative language. "Through infirmity of the flesh," δι᾿ ἀσθένειαν τῆς
σαρκός· The preposition may here have the meaning of, 'along with,' or,
'under the circumstances or influence of, in the condition of.' Robinson in his Lexicon, II. 1. b), classes it under the category " of external circumstances operating as a motive, cause, or occasion," and translates "because of weakness." In the work of Conybeare and Howson this view is
pretty fully developed. "It was sickness which caused me to preach the
glad tidings to you:" vol. ii. p. 146. In chap. ix. vol. i. p. 294, we have
the same view: "It was bodily sickness which caused St. Paul to preach to
the Galatians at the first. The allusion is to his first visit, and the obvious inference is that he was passing through Galatia to some other district,
when the state of his bodily health arrested his progress." What may be
"obvious" to one reader, another may be utterly incompetent to dis-
cern. The writer adds in a note: "There can be no doubt that the literal
translation is on account of bodily weakness." Ellicott also decides that

14 ρον, καὶ τὸν πειρασμόν μου τὸν   my temptation which was in my
ἐν τῇ σαρκί μου οὐκ ἐξουθενή-   flesh ye despised not, nor rejected:

" the only grammatically correct translation is, *on account of bodily infirm-ity ;*" although he admits " that the line of demarkation between διά with gen. and with accus. is sometimes so faint, that in some few passages an interchange seems really to have taken place." Instead, however, of making sickness the cause or occasion of St. Paul's original preaching to the Galatians, he considers the "bodily weakness" referred to as merely "obliging him to stay longer with the Galatians than he intended." Still he translates thus: " It was on account of infirmity of the flesh that I preached the Gospel unto you the first time."

No doubt the common meaning of διά with an accusative is *on account of;* and of this usage we have a striking illustration in Heb. ii. 10. Jowett remarks that, " in the explanation of διά we have to choose between ordi-nary Greek usage and the sense of the passage ;" which remark pre-sumes the sense to be either self evident, or known in some other way than ordinary usage.   Certainly, as he proceeds to say, " of mere sickness St. Paul would hardly have used such strong language as ἐξεπτύσατε, which seems to imply something perhaps painful, perhaps ridiculous, such as would naturally move the disgust of mankind."   To this it may be added that what the Apostle calls " temptation" or "infirmity of the flesh," was evidently something which adhered to him while he was preaching among the Galatians.   Therefore, it could not have been an attack of illness, for in this case, he must have recovered in order to have become able to preach.   Although the sense of διά as above given is the most usual, yet it is certainly not invariable.   In John vi. 57, the translation *on account of,* would give an intelligible and sound meaning, but one not at all adapted to the context, which requires the sense of *by,* although the noun is in the accusative.   Ellicott remarks :   " It is far from impossible that St. John designedly used διά with the accus. as expressing more nearly the theo-logical shade of meaning he wished to convey than διά with the genitive." But what "theological shade of meaning" he supposes to be intended he does not state.   In Rev. xii. 11 and xiii. 14 also, διά with the accusative is much more naturally translated, " *by* the blood of the lamb, *by* the word, *by* those miracles," than *on account of.*   Certainly, as Jowett remarks, St. Paul " is describing *the state in which* he (was when he) preached to the Galatians ; not *some accidental cause* of his mission."   He proclaimed it when under the influence of bodily infirmities.   Compare Phil. i. 15, διὰ φθόνον καὶ ἔριν—δι' εὐδοκίαν, which is equivalent to, ' influenced by envy and contention—by good will.'   The only difference in the cases is that the one expresses *motive,* the other, *a state or condition which was practical in its influence.*

" At the first :"   This has been thought to intimate that the Apostle had

but received me as an angel of God,   σατε οὐδὲ ἐξεπτύσατε, ἀλλ᾽ ὡς
                                      ἄγγελον Θεοῦ ἐδέξασθέ με, ὡς

visited the Galatians twice.   The opinion agrees with a comparison of Acts
xvi. 6 and xviii. 23, from which it appears that the latter text relates a
second visit.   See the Introduction.

"My temptation," or 'trial:' The received reading of which this is the
translation, has the pronoun μου.   The meaning is perfectly natural and
needs no exposition.   But ὑμῶν 'your,' is well supported on external
evidence, and not without analogous usage.   According to it St. Paul represents his own bodily infirmity as a trial to the Galatians, whose apostle
he had become.   What the "temptation" or rather 'trial' was of which he
here speaks, it is impossible to say with certainty.   It were idle to explain
it of persecutions, for those he would never speak of as physical infirmity.
And equally idle is it to imagine that it consisted of a weakness of the
eyes, occasioned by the remains of the impression made on him by the
bright light that blinded him previous to his conversion, and to suppose an
allusion to this diseased condition in the next verse.   That it was some
corporeal affection is rendered probable by his speaking of a physical infirmity which made his enemies ridicule "his bodily presence as weak
and his speech contemptible:" 2 Cor. x. 10.   Perhaps it was identical
with what, in 2 Cor. xii. 7, he calls "a thorn in the flesh."   The connection
in which this phrase stands seems to intimate that it denotes some bodily
affection occasioned by the frequency and character of the revelations with
which the Apostle was favored : " Lest I should be exalted above measure
through the abundance of the revelations, there was given to me a thorn in
the flesh, the messenger of Satan to buffet me."   That divine communications should produce powerful effects on the physical frame is in itself altogether probable, and the opinion has the sanction of high authority.   Maimonides, the most distinguished of the Jewish Rabbies, speaking of prophets,
uses this language: "When they prophesy, their limbs tremble, and their
physical strength fails.   As it is said of Abraham, a horror of great dark-
ness fell upon him; and of Daniel, my comeliness was turned in me into
corruption and I retained no strength."   And again, when discoursing on
the prophetic vision : "It is a fearful thing, producing terror, which seizes
the prophet in a time when he is awake, as it is evidently stated in Daniel,
where he says: and I saw this great vision, and there remained no strength
in me, for my comeliness was turned in me into corruption, and I retained
no strength."*   This certainly agrees with the representations made by the
beloved prophet.   "I was afraid and fell upon my face: I Daniel faint-
ed and was sick certain days: my sorrows are turned upon me and I
have retained no strength." †   If therefore such extraordinary revelations as

---

* See Jewish Rabbies, pp. 217, 229.   † Dan. viii. 17, 27. x. 16.

15 Χριστὸν Ἰησοῦν. Ποῦ οὖν ὁ μακαρισμὸς ὑμῶν; μαρτυρῶ γὰρ ὑμῖν, ὅτι εἰ δυνατόν, τοὺς ὀφθαλ-μοὺς ὑμῶν ἐξορύξαντες ἂν ἐδώ-

even as Christ Jesus. Where is 15 then the blessedness ye spake of? for I bear you record, that, if *it had been* possible, ye would have plucked out your own eyes, and

were made to the favored Apostle did exert a permanent or long continued influence on his nervous system, which subjected him to pain and exposed him at times even to the ridicule of the silly, this would accord with scriptural analogy. If the phrase "Satan's messenger," which is employed to describe this result, be thought inconsistent with the opinion, it may be sufficient to remark that such language does not necessarily imply belief in Satan's agency in producing the distress thus denominated. It may have been in current use in the Apostle's time, and thus similar to the popular expressions, "St. Vitus' dance" or "St. Anthony's fire," occasionally heard in the present day. But every one knows that this phraseology is employed without the least idea of supernatural agency in reference to these respective diseases.

"Ye received me as an angel of God, even as Christ Jesus :" The deep reverence with which the Galatians regarded the Apostle is forcibly expressed by this language, part of which is borrowed from Old Testament usage. Thus Achish addresses David : "Thou art good in my sight as an angel of God :" 1 Sam. xxix. 9; and the woman of Tekoah tells him that he is "as an angel of God :" 2 Sam. xiv. 17.

15. "Blessedness :" That is, the happy condition. See Rom. iv. 6, 9. "Where is then," etc. Instead of τίς, our translators read ποῦ, which is supported by considerable external authority, although τίς is admitted into most of the critical editions. Olshausen prefers ποῦ. The verb ἦν, *was*, which follows in the received text, makes a difficulty, and therefore most probably it was stricken out of some ancient manuscripts which want it. Ποῦ, where, requires the present tense, which our translation employs. Either reading makes a very good meaning : 'Where is your former happy condition?' or, 'what was it!' What a blessed state! How favored you regarded yourselves! "I bear you record that, if possible, ye would have plucked out your own eyes and have given them to me." It is extraordinary that Conybeare should regard these words as "certainly seeming to confirm the view of those who suppose St. Paul's malady to have been some disease in the eyes." They merely denote the delightful eagerness with which the grateful Galatians would have deprived themselves of anything, however useful and precious, to benefit the beloved spiritual father. The expression may have been proverbial. Compare the language of Horace : Eripiet quivis oculos citius mihi quam, etc.*

* Satires, Lib. II. Sat. V. 35.

16 have given them to me. Am I
therefore become your enemy, be-
17 cause I tell you the truth? They
zealously affect you, *but* not well;
yea, they would exclude you, that
18 ye might affect them. But *it is*
good to be zealously affected always in a good *thing*, and not only

κατέ μοι. Ὥστε ἐχϑρὸς ὑμῶν 16
γέγονα ἀληϑεύων ὑμῖν; Ζηλοῦ- 17
σιν ὑμᾶς οὐ καλῶς, ἀλλὰ ἐκκλεῖ-
σαι ὑμᾶς ϑέλουσιν, ἵνα αὐτοὺς
ζηλοῦτε. Καλὸν δὲ τὸ ζηλοῦσ- 18
ϑαι ἐν καλῷ πάντοτε, καὶ μὴ
μόνον ἐν τῷ παρεῖναί με πρὸς

---

16. This verse may be read so as to express the Apostle's surprise and
amazement, at the result of placing the truth before the minds of the Galatians; but the interrogative form is simpler and preferable.

17, 18. Ζηλόω means 'to show or take much interest in, to appear or be
zealous for.' In the second clause, the true reading is ὑμᾶς, " you," not
ἡμᾶς, us, which appears in the margin of our English translation. De
Wette indeed decides in favor of the latter reading; but chiefly because
in his opinion it "gives the best sense," and the interpretations founded
on the former are all "more or less arbitrary." Such argument ought not
to be allowed to set aside a reading supported by the best manuscripts
and versions. Ἵνα is here followed by the indicative, as it is also in the
second instance in which it occurs in 1 Cor. iv. 6. Perhaps in both cases
it is a slight grammatical inaccuracy. "They wish to exclude you;"
meaning, either from fellowship with me, which would be the natural result
of devoted attachment to Jewish exclusive rites, or from connection with
the church and its blessings, a termination to which such bigoted attachment would as naturally tend. The sense of the whole verse will become
the clearer by placing the middle part of it in a parenthesis, thus : 'They
affect a great zeal for you, (not well, not honorably, but they desire to exclude you,) in order that you may cherish a zeal for them;' that is, their zeal
towards you is both hypocritical and selfish. The parenthetical portion
shows how injurious it might become to the Galatians. In the next verse
ζηλοῦσϑαι may perhaps be middle, equivalent to ζηλοῦν, to have a zeal for.
Locke maintains that καλῷ should be rendered, a good man, and that the
Apostle must mean himself, of whom he had just spoken as having been
greatly beloved by the Galatians, whose attachment to him had been
cooled in his absence by the influence of false teachers. To this he thinks
the Apostle alludes in the words, "always and not only when I am present
with you," and that he urges them, if he is the good man that they suppose him to be, to continue their attachment even during his absence.
But it does not well accord with St. Paul's modesty to suppose that he
would thus distinguish himself; and it is quite natural that he should take
this occasion to lay down a general principle, namely, that we should be
zealous in a good cause under all circumstances.—Ellicott, who says that

19 ὑμᾶς· τεκνία μου, οὓς πάλιν
ὠδίνω, ἄχρις οὗ μορφωθῇ Χρισ-
20 τὸς ἐν ὑμῖν· ἤθελον δὲ παρεῖ-
ναι πρὸς ὑμᾶς ἄρτι καὶ ἀλλάξαι
τὴν φωνήν μου, ὅτι ἀποροῦμαι
ἐν ὑμῖν.

when I am present with you. My 19
little children, of whom I travail
in birth again until Christ be formed in you, I desire to be present 20
with you now, and to change my
voice; for I stand in doubt of you.

"ζηλοῦσθαι cannot be taken as a middle equivalent in sense to active," regards the clause ζηλοῦσθαι ἐν καλῷ as " in strict antithesis to the active
ζηλοῦσιν οὐ καλῶς." He translates thus : "They pay you court, in no
honest way," etc. " But it is good to be courted in honesty at all times,"
etc. Thus he regards the verb as in the passive.

19. Τεκνία μου· The neuter is followed by the masculine οὓς, which
refers to them as sons. Compare Matt. xxviii. 19, and Rom. ix. 22–24,
where ἔθνη is followed by αὐτούς and σκεύη by οὓς. " My little children :" Rather, ' my dear children,' for the appellation is evidently one of
affection. Thus our Lord seems to employ it in John xiii. 33. Also St.
John, in his first Epistle ii. 12, where it comprehends true Christians in
general, and is followed by terms designating their religious ages and
standing. See also ver. 28 of the same chapter and elsewhere in the Epistle. St. Paul addresses the Galatian converts with extreme tenderness. In
speaking of the anguish he endures in his efforts to bring them back again
to a true Christian state and character, he employs a figure taken from a
mother's distress in her condition preparatory to childbirth. The meaning
is beautifully illustrated by Koppe : " O my dear children, in forming
whom anew I struggle with the care and solicitude of a pregnant mother,
I will spare no distress, no labor, until ye become formed into genuine
and perfect followers of Christ."—The word again seems to allude to the
Apostle's original efforts in effecting their conversion.

20. Ἤθελον, the imperfect, is probably used for the optative, as in
Rom. ix. 3 and Acts xxv. 22, and may be translated, ' I could wish.'—
" To change my voice :" This may mean, ' to use a milder strain of representation and entreaty than that which generally pervades the Epistle ;' or,
' to adapt myself, both in the subject and manner of my addresses, to the
different states of mind which prevail among various classes.'

SECTION IV.

Chap. IV. 21—V. 12.

THE INCONSISTENCY OF FALLING BACK UPON THE LAW FOR JUSTIFICATION
AND ACCEPTANCE WITH GOD, ILLUSTRATED BY AN ALLEGORICAL APPLI-
CATION OF A PART OF ABRAHAM'S HISTORY.   CORRESPONDING EXHORT-
ATIONS AND WARNINGS.

21 Tell me, ye that desire to be under the law, do ye not hear the law?
22 For it is written, that Abraham had two sons; the one by a bond-maid, the other by a free woman.
23 But he *who was* of the bond woman was born after the flesh; but he of the free woman *was* by pro-
24 mise. Which things are an allegory: for these are the two cov-

Λέγετέ μοι, οἱ ὑπὸ νόμον 21
θέλοντες εἶναι, τὸν νόμον οὐκ
ἀκούετε; Γέγραπται γάρ, ὅτι 22
Ἀβραὰμ δύο υἱοὺς ἔσχεν, ἕνα
ἐκ τῆς παιδίσκης καὶ ἕνα ἐκ τῆς
ἐλευθέρας. Ἀλλ' ὁ μὲν ἐκ τῆς 23
παιδίσκης κατὰ σάρκα γεγέννη-
ται, ὁ δὲ ἐκ τῆς ἐλευθέρας διὰ
τῆς ἐπαγγελίας. Ἅτινά ἐστιν 24
ἀλληγορούμενα· αὗται γάρ εἰσιν

21. THE word "law," as first employed, means the Mosaic system chiefly as one of outward observances.   Immediately afterward it denotes the Old Testament, or that part of it which contains an account of that system and what preceded its establishment, the religion of which period was most probably characterised in general by external services.—"Ye who desire:" Θέλοντες here implies the inclination and tendency of the whole mind, as in John viii. 44, "the lusts of your father ye *will* do;" Acts vii. 39, "whom they *would* not obey;" Gal. i. 7 and Col. ii. 18, 'bent upon overthrowing, *bent* upon humility.'—"Hear:" attend to, consider, in which sense the word is often used.

The Apostle then proceeds to give the allegorical bearing of certain facts in the life of Abraham.   He mentions the birth of his two sons; Ishmael, whose mother was Hagar the Egyptian bondwoman, and who was born according to the ordinary course of nature, and Isaac, the child of his old and legitimate wife Sarah.   The birth of this son in the advanced age of his parents was the extraordinary result of God's particular promise, and therefore, in ver. 29, is said to have been "after the Spirit," that is, not in the usual but in a miraculous way.   Of these children and their respective mothers, and the condition of all the parties, he speaks as follows.

24, 25. "Which things are an allegory:" This is, no doubt, a very

δύο διαθῆκαι· μία μὲν ἀπὸ ὄρους   enants; the one from the mount
Σινᾶ, εἰς δουλείαν γεννῶσα, ἥτις   Sinai, which gendereth to bondage,

---

loose and inaccurate translation. The Greek will not bear it, nor does the idea which it naturally suggests meet with any encouragement from St. Paul's writings. He never represents the historical parts of the Old Testament as allegories. The French version of De Sacy gives the same view: Tout ceci est une allégorie. Martin's is better: Or, ces choses doivent être entendues par allégorie; "these things must be understood by way of allegory." The Vulgate has: quæ sunt per allegoriam dicta; and this is followed by Cranmer and the Rhemish: "Which thynges are spoken by an allegorye—which thynges are said by an allegorie." Wiclif renders thus: "The whiche thingis ben seide bi anothir undirstondinge;" and to the same purpose the Geneva version: "By the which thinges another thing is meant." Tyndale has: "Which things betoken mystery." Luther: "The words mean (or betoken) something," die Wörte bedeuten etwas. The translation of Diodati is very good: "Which things have an allegorical sense:" Le quale cose hanno un senso allegorico. The definition which Suidas gives of allegory seems to have suggested some of these translations: "Allegory is a metaphor, where one thing is said and another intended."

Koppe states the two views of which the words are susceptible. St. Paul may mean that, in the narrative of Moses, something quite different from the merely historical statement was intended; or, that the narrative may be taken in a much more elevated sense than the historical one, and accommodated to the Apostle's purpose. He argues in favor of the latter view, because in merely historical narratives, as those in the Pentateuch, no clear instances of similar allegory can be alleged; and further, because this method of allegorizing even historical accounts was common with the ancients. Stanley also, in his long but very unsatisfactory note on 1 Cor. xv. 29, affirms that St. Paul's reasoning in Galatians is "founded on the allegorical interpretation of the Old Testament, and accommodated to the feelings and opinions of those addressed." Thus, it is said, the Platonists and other Greek philosophers interpreted Homer. The Jews also had adopted the same method of allegorical exposition, and applied it to this very narrative, of which we have a remarkable illustration in Philo, and afterwards in the Christian father Clement of Alexandria.* The Apostle therefore does but imitate their example.—The latter re-

---

* It may be well, by way of contrast to the very natural allegory drawn out by the Apostle, to give the reader some intimation of the use made of this narrative by the authors referred to. Clement is defending the importance of cultivating the whole circle of human learning, and especially philosophy. He endeavors to sustain his position by an allegorical representation of this account of Abraham's paternity. ˙His wife Sarah was a long time barren, and at last gave her maiden Hagar to her husband. The patriarch is the image of the faithful and just man, and his wife of wisdom. Wisdom dwells in

25 which is Agar, (for this Agar is   ἐστὶν Ἄγαρ· (τὸ γὰρ Ἄγαρ 25
mount Sinai in Arabia :) and an-   Σινᾶ ὄρος ἐστὶν ἐν τῇ Ἀραβίᾳ·)

---

marks only prove what was usual with Greeks and Jews. The statement
made in Koppe's first argument may be regarded as doubtful, to say
the least. The fact that Moses was not allowed to conduct the Israelites
into the promised land, and that this office was reserved for Joshua,
appears to have been intended to illustrate allegorically the important
truth, that the law could not secure admission into heaven, to effect
which the efforts and guidance of the Saviour were required. And
other facts have been thought to be susceptible of similar allegorical
exposition. It is clear that the Apostle does represent the facts referred
to as designed, in the same manner as parables, to convey religious
instruction. It has been supposed by some, that he does himself intimate to the reader his intention of accommodating to the Jewish usage in
the application which he is about to make of the facts immediately re-
counted. This intimation, they think, is conveyed in the 20th verse, where
he expresses his desire to " change his voice." This is assumed to mean,
to alter his general method of instruction, or to adapt himself to each one's
thought and feeling, thus condescending to the erroneous use of allegory
in accommodation to their Jewish weakness and prejudice.* But this application of the clause is forced and unnatural. The author's question in
ver. 21, " do ye not hear the law ?" that is, ' do ye not perceive and attend
to what the Scripture itself intimates ?' evidently shows that he not only
considered the instruction which he was about to convey as implied in the
facts recorded, but that his readers might themselves have drawn from the
record some such instruction. In a word, he regards Sarah and her son as
prefigurative of the Christian church and its spiritual members, while
Hagar and Ishmael represent the Jewish community devoted to an external religion, which was characterised by elementary principles, mere
rites and ceremonies of a fleshly nature. Such a view of these facts is in

intimate connection with the faithful man, but remains childless, producing nothing excellent for
Abraham. But, having devoted himself to the learning of the world, (for Egypt allegorically interpreted signifies the world,) [he means having had connection with the Egyptian Hagar,] afterwards,
through divine Providence, by intercourse with her, [Sarah, the true mistress of wisdom,] he becomes
the father of Isaac.' In other words, this portion of Abraham's history shows that, to make advances
in the knowledge of divine things, and to extend and propagate this knowledge, previous devotion to
the circle of human knowledge and acquisition of it are necessary. Stromata, Lib. i. p. 284, Opera,
Edit. Sylburg. Lutet. 1629. Philo allegorizes in a similar strain : ' Hagar, a stranger sojourning in the
family, symbolizes learning in general. Sarah, equivalent to *my princess* or *ruler*, is the perfect,
ruling virtue of the soul; and we cannot receive progeny of virtue, unless we first have intercourse
with the maid servant, that is, the circle of preparatory instruction.' See the passages in Koppe in loc.
It is impossible not to feel how vapid and senseless is such trifling compared with the judicious and
tasteful analogy drawn out by St. Paul. Compare what is said on this subject in the note on
Heb. viii. 1.
  * See HAHN's Lehrbuch des Christlichen Glaubens, § 14, Anm. 2, p. 65; and his Treatise on the
Grammatico-Historical Interpretation of the Scriptures, in the Biblical Repository, vol. i. No. 1, p. 138.

συστοιχεῖ δὲ τῇ νῦν Ἰερουσαλήμ,   swereth to Jerusalem which now
δουλεύει γὰρ μετὰ τῶν τέκνων   is, and is in bondage with her child-

---

harmony with the scriptural representation of the connection of the old
and new covenants, which is illustrated by the doctrine that the one was
intended to be symbolical of the other. The particulars here stated of the
life of Abraham furnish a suitable comparison with the points to which the
Apostle applies them. Thus, as Hagar's offspring was born in a state of
servitude, so the Jews were subjected to the ritual law. As Isaac, the son
of the free woman, was himself free, so are Christians free from the Jewish
yoke. And as the two children were born, the one according to nature
and in his behavior showed his natural character, and the other by virtue
of the divine promise, so unbelieving Jews are in their natural sinful condition and act accordingly, while true Christians are born of the Spirit, and
persecuted by their blinded opponents.

"These are the two covenants:" We have here a striking instance of
the use of the substantive verb in the sense of *signify*. This is so common
that it would be superfluous to give examples. The usage bears upon
the meaning of the words, "this is my body," in the institution of the
Lord's supper.—The word Ἄγαρ in ver. 25 is omitted in some ancient
manuscripts and versions, but it is undoubtedly genuine, and was probably
stricken out on account of a supposed difficulty, or overlooked through
the haste of some transcriber from its similarity to τὸ γάρ, which immediately precedes it, leaving the reading thus : ' for Sinai is a mountain in
Arabia.' Some critics, influenced by the former reason, have rejected the
whole clause, but the weight of external authority is entirely in its favor.
The simplest construction of the passage is that which places this clause
in a parenthesis, and connects ver. 24 with the remainder of ver. 25,
thus : ' The one indeed from mount Sinai, bringing forth its offspring in a
state of bondage, which is Hagar, and she corresponds with the present
Jerusalem.' The intermediate clause contains merely an illustration drawn
from the meaning and application of the word *hagar* in Arabic. The
neuter article τό, which immediately follows the feminine pronoun ἥτις,
shows that the word and not the woman is what is meant. In Arabic
the word *hajaroun*, (the final syllable is the Arabic termination, and the
pronunciation of the j is soft,) signifies a stone or rock.* The rocky character of Mount Sinai would make the application of such a term particularly appropriate, and that it was so applied we have the authority of

---

* See Freytag's Arabic Lexicon under the word, vol. i. pp. 345, 346. Among various other meanings he gives the following: In the 5th conjugation, to turn to stone, to petrify; in the 8th, to be
stony ; as a noun, a stone, a dark stone, a place abounding with stones or rocks. Golius, under חגר,
Col. 255, 256, a stone, a rock, a stony or rocky place.—"The famous city of Idumea, Petra, 'the
Rock city,' is in Arabic *Elhhagar*." Olshausen.

26 ren. But Jerusalem which is	αὐτῆς· ἡ δὲ ἄνω Ἰερουσαλὴμ 26
above is free, which is the mother	ἐλευθέρα ἐστίν, ἥτις ἐστὶ μήτηρ
27 of us all. For it is written, Rejoice	[πάντων] ἡμῶν. Γέγραπται γάρ· 27

Chrysostom,* Œcumenius† and Theophylact,‡ in loc. Büsching, in his Description of the Rocky Arabia, states from the traveller Haranti, that this word was applied by the Arabians to mount Sinai.§ St. Paul may have acquired a knowledge of its meaning and application during the time that he spent in Arabia, (see i. 17,) and it is perfectly natural that he should in this connection avail himself of his knowledge. See Koppe's Excursus VIII. p. 137. The Apostle does not argue from the analogy of the name of Ishmael's mother with the rocky mountain which was the awful scene of the promulgation of the law; he only states it as a remarkable coincidence, as he does also the names of Melchisedek and Salem, with their respective meanings, in Heb. vii. 3. As no argument is founded on the remark, which merely states an analogy of expression, it is the less surprising that he should refer to the Arabic word, although its first letter corresponds with the Hebrew *cheth*, while the name of Abraham's bondwoman begins with a *he*, and has the meaning of *flight*.‖ Borger, in a note appended to his comment on this passage, shows that in the oriental dialects the words for mountain and rock are often used interchangeably : pp. 306–308.

In the received text δέ occurs after δουλεύει. But the weight of evidence, both from ancient manuscripts and versions, decides in favor of γάρ. Koppe has no doubt that this was introduced as a correction of δέ, and therefore rejects it. But in addition to the external argument, it may be urged that it makes the comparison still clearer : 'for the present Jerusalem is in bondage with her children, as Hagar and Ishmael also were.'— 'The present Jerusalem with her children' is a figurative expression for, the Jewish church and its members. The former clause represents it in the aggregate, the latter in its individuals. We have similar usage in Isa. l. 1, where the mother and the children addressed represent the same body thus differently considered. The same remark applies to the view given in Hos. i.

26, 27. "But the Jerusalem which is above is free, which is the mother of us all :" The last word is wanting in some of the best manuscripts; also in the Syriac and other ancient versions. It was probably added for the sake of emphasis, in order to comprehend all true Christians, Gentiles

---

* Comment. ad Gal. cap. iv. sect. 8, end. Op. Tom. x. p. 710.
† In Gal. cap. ix, Op. tom. i. p. 755, Edit. Paris. 1631.
‡ Op. tom. ii. p. 852.
§ Erdbeschreibung, Eleventh Part, Hamburg, 1792, p. 603.
‖ Hence the term *Hegira*, applied by the Mohammedans to mark their era, from the *flight* of their prophet from Mecca.

εὐφράνθητι στεῖρα ἡ οὐ τίκτου-
σα, ῥῆξον καὶ βόησον ἡ οὐκ ὠδί-
νουσα· ὅτι πολλὰ τὰ τέκνα τῆς
ἐρήμου μᾶλλον ἢ τῆς ἐχούσης

thou barren that bearest not; break
forth and cry, thou that travailest
not; for the desolate hath many
more children than she which hath

---

as well as the Jews, and to agree more closely with the quotation which immediately follows.—The sentence is elliptical. The comparison of Hagar
and her offspring with the Jewish community was drawn out in detail; that
of Sarah and her son is merely suggested. But any intelligent reader can
easily supply what is omitted. This is done by Koppe, and nearly in these
terms: 'And the other covenant produceth its children in a state of freedom, which is Sarah, and she corresponds with the Jerusalem which is
above, which is free and our mother.' The *above* or heavenly Jerusalem
is antithetic to the Jerusalem that *now* is, and the phrase was chosen doubtless in order to express the more vividly the contrast between the temporary, preparative, Jewish dispensation, and the whole state and condition
of the Christian church both here and hereafter. In the same way in Heb.
xii. 22, 18, "mount Zion, the city of the living God, the heavenly Jerusalem," are contrasted with "the mount that might be touched, and that
burned with fire," the two dispensations being thus depicted. The phrases,
'the Jerusalem above' and 'the Jerusalem below,' ירושלם של מעלה, or
למעלה, ירושלם של מטה are found in the Rabbies, and are used to denote the
Jewish church or state or kingdom here on earth, and the celestial kingdom of the Messiah. Thus we read in the Talmud, Treatise Taanith, that
is, of Fasts, Col. 5, 1: "Says Rabbi Johanan, God said, I will not enter
into the Jerusalem which is above, ירושלם של מעלה, until I go to the Jerusalem which is below, של מטה ר'.* The language here employed is equivalent to that constantly occurring in the Gospels, "the kingdom of heaven."
The name of the holy city is used figuratively to denote the whole community of the people of the Messiah as existing in his church on earth and
also in their state of future happiness. Similar language occurs in other
writings of St. Paul, although it does not always appear in our translation.
Thus in Phil. iii. 14, the original for "high calling" is 'the above calling,'
that is, the Christian state and condition, which is from above, celestial in
origin, character and destination. Hence Christians are exhorted to 'seek
and to mind the things above,' Col. iii. 1, 2; and "the new Jerusalem"
appears to St. John in vision, as "coming down from God out of heaven."
See Rev. xxi. 2, and compare iii. 12. This view comprehends the two
meanings, between the choice of which Borger says he for a long time hes-
itated. It ought ever to be kept in mind that the sacred writers regard

---

* See Wetstein in loc. for other illustrations; also Schoettgen, de Hieros. cœlest., appended to his
Horæ Hebraicæ, p. 1210, and Bertholdt de Christologia Judæorum, § 46, p. 217.

28 a husband. Now we, brethren, as Isaac was, are the children of
29 promise. But as then he that was born after the flesh persecuted him *that was born* after the Spirit, even

τὸν ἄνδρα. Ἡμεῖς δέ, ἀδελφοί, 28 κατὰ Ἰσαὰκ ἐπαγγελίας τέκνα ἐσμέν. Ἀλλ' ὥσπερ τότε ὁ κατὰ 29 σάρκα γεννηθεὶς ἐδίωκε τὸν κατὰ πνεῦμα, οὕτω καὶ νῦν.

Messiah's kingdom as commencing indeed on earth, yet continuing in all subsequent stages of the existence of his followers, both with "the spirits of just men made perfect" and "with Christ," (Heb. xii. 23, Phil. i. 23,) before the general resurrection, and also in that "everlasting kingdom" (2 Pet. i. 11,) of future glory to which his true members shall finally be admitted.

There is no reason to suppose, as Macknight assumes, that Isaiah, in liv. 1, the place here quoted, addresses himself to Sarah. The felicity to be expected in the Messiah's kingdom, and the vast extent of that kingdom, increasing by manifold accessions of converted Gentiles as well as Jews, are the thoughts which he has in view. These he describes under the figure of a woman who had been repudiated by her husband, and again received into favor, and who unexpectedly finds herself the happy mother of numerous offspring. Τὸν ἄνδρα· The accurate translation is, 'the husband,' whose return to his formerly rejected wife is implied. The article should not be ignored. It may be equivalent in meaning to the personal pronoun. The quotation is made in order to illustrate what had just been said, namely, that the heavenly Jerusalem, the Christian church, is the mother of believers. It agrees with the Septuagint.

28. "Children of promise:" This does not merely signify 'promised children,' those whose being verifies the divine promise to the ancient forsaken church; but rather, children by virtue of the promise. The analogy between the birth of Isaac in consequence of the particular promise of God and therefore by a special divine influence, and the new birth of the believer by the agency of God's Spirit, is the point here stated.

29. "After the Spirit:" As this phrase is antithetic to, "after the flesh," it must be equivalent to, "by," that is, by virtue of "the promise," in ver. 23. The words Spirit and spiritual are often employed to denote what is peculiar, extraordinary, superior.—"Persecuted:" This view of Ishmael's conduct towards Isaac is sanctioned by Jewish tradition. Some of the Rabbies say that Sarah had observed in Ishmael a disposition to idolatry, lasciviousness, and other vices. But this is probably nothing but a fiction, founded in national prejudice, and perhaps in the fact that the Hebrew word rendered "mocking" in Gen. xxi. 9, is sometimes used in connection with such wickedness. Others, with more probability, suppose that Ishmael claimed the right of inheritance as being the elder son; and

30 Ἀλλὰ τί λέγει ἡ γραφή; ἔκβαλε   so *it is* now. Nevertheless what 30
τὴν παιδίσκην καὶ τὸν υἱὸν   saith the Scripture? Cast out the
αὐτῆς· οὐ γὰρ μὴ κληρονομήσῃ   bond-woman and her son: for the
ὁ υἱὸς τῆς παιδίσκης μετὰ τοῦ   son of the bond-woman shall not

---

this agrees with ver. 10, "the son of this bond-woman shall not be heir with my son, with Isaac." See Munster, Drusius, Notæ Majores, and Cartwright, in the Critici Sacri. St. Paul's representation is, at least, in harmony with the Old Testament account. That the conduct of Hagar towards Sarah was insolent is evident from Gen. xvi. 4, 5, and most probably she instilled her own feeling into the mind of her son, whose natural character would prompt him to show hostility to those whom he disliked: ver. 12. The word translated "mocking" in xxi. 9, מְצַחֵק, is derived from the same root as Isaac and might be rendered 'laughing at, insulting.' It is used to express the grossest degree of insult, as in the false accusation of Potiphar's wife against Joseph, "the Hebrew servant came in unto me to *mock me:*" xxxix. 14, 17. Although the supposition of personal violence in the case of Ishmael and Isaac is wholly out of the question, yet something insulting, and perhaps malicious and infidel, may fairly be inferred from the circumstances. "He did not merely laugh," says Hengstenberg,[*] "he made himself merry. The little helpless Isaac, a father of nations! Unbelief, jealousy, pride, led him to this behavior. Want of faith made it appear to him ridiculous, to connect such great results with such a feeble cause."

Jowett's remarks on the latter portion of this chapter are quite unsatisfactory, and indeed in part without any foundation. What the Apostle here explains as persecution on the part of Ishmael, this writer represents as a "simple statement that Sarah saw him 'playing' with her son Isaac,— the word for which neither in the Hebrew nor the LXX admits the sense of mocking." How little such declarations are to be relied on must be evident from the texts above cited.

30. "What saith the Scripture?" See this same formula, in Rom. iv. 3, xi. 2, and compare x. 8, and xi. 4. The application here made of the language of Sarah in Gen. xxi. 10, is somewhat similar to that in Heb. xiii. 13. The law required the body of the victim, whose blood the high priest on the great day of atonement had sprinkled in the most holy place, to be burned without the camp: See Levit. xvi. 27. In accordance with this law Jesus made the propitiatory offering of himself without the precincts of the city. This analogy the Apostle then practically applies, exhorting his readers to abandon Judaism and every such imperfect system by believing on and adhering to Christ. And so here he denounces the Jewish system

---

* Authentie des Pentateuches, vol. i, p. 276.

be heir with the son of the free
31 woman. So then, brethren, we are
not children of the bond-woman,
but of the free.

V.   Stand fast therefore in the liberty
wherewith Christ hath made us
free, and be not entangled again
2 with the yoke of bondage. Behold, I Paul say unto you, that if
ye be circumcised, Christ shall pro-
3 fit you nothing. For I testify again
to every man that is circumcised,
that he is a debtor to do the whole

υἱοῦ τῆς ἐλευθέρας· Ἄρα, ἀδελ- 31
φοί, οὐκ ἐσμὲν παιδίσκης τέκνα, ἀλλὰ τῆς ἐλευθέρας.

Τῇ ἐλευθερίᾳ ᾗ ἡμᾶς Χριστὸς V.
ἠλευθέρωσε στήκετε οὖν, καὶ μὴ
πάλιν ζυγῷ δουλείας ἐνέχεσθε.
Ἴδε, ἐγὼ Παῦλος λέγω ὑμῖν, ὅτι 2
ἐὰν περιτέμνησθε, Χριστὸς ὑμᾶς
οὐδὲν ὠφελήσει· μαρτύρομαι δὲ 3
πάλιν παντὶ ἀνθρώπῳ περιτεμ-
νομένῳ, ὅτι ὀφειλέτης ἐστὶν
ὅλον τὸν νόμον ποιῆσαι. Κατηρ- 4

as securing to its adherents no claim to Christian privileges and the divine
inheritance, and, in the words of Abraham's incensed wife, urges the Galatians to reject it. For a vindication of the patriarch's conduct towards
Hagar and Ishmael, the reader is referred to my companion to Genesis,
pp. 283, 284.

31. This inference founded on the preceding allegorical representation
is merely a repetition of what had been before said.—Ellicott's translation
keeps in view the absence and presence respectively of the article : "We
are not children of *a* bondwoman but of *the* free."

v. 1. This verse is so closely connected as a practical inference with
what precedes, that it ought not to have been separated therefrom as the
commencement of a new chapter.—Several various readings are nearly
equally sustained by external authority, as may be seen in Griesbach and
other critical editions; but the general meaning of each is the same. The
tenor of the exhortation is to be firm in maintaining that freedom from the
ritual law, which Christ, by abolishing it, hath secured for us. See Eph. ii.
14, 15, Col. ii. 14, 20, 21.—"Entangled :" literally, held in, restrained.
The word is applied to fetters, laws, restraints of various kinds. 'Op-
pressed' agrees best with the figure of a yoke.

2–4. In order to give impression to his declaration, St. Paul adds his
own name. This seems to indicate that, notwithstanding the hostility of
the false teachers, the weight of the Apostle's authority was still recognised,
at least by many of the Galatian Christians. It is possible, however,
that by introducing his own name he calls their attention to his Apostolic authority, intimating at the same time the absurdity of the charge
which had been brought against him of advocating circumcision and other
Jewish rites. "If ye be circumcised :" That is, if ye submit to circumcision, regarding it as essential to justification with God. The word is emphatic, like "worketh" in Rom. iv. 5, which means worketh with a view

γήθητε ἀπὸ τοῦ Χριστοῦ, οἵτι-
νες ἐν νόμῳ δικαιοῦσθε· τῆς
5 χάριτος ἐξεπέσατε. Ἡμεῖς γὰρ
πνεύματι ἐκ πίστεως ἐλπίδα
6 δικαιοσύνης ἀπεκδεχόμεθα. Ἐν
γὰρ Χριστῷ Ἰησοῦ οὔτε περιτομή τι ἰσχύει οὔτε ἀκροβυστία,
ἀλλὰ πίστις δι' ἀγάπης ἐνεργου-

law. Christ is become of no 4
effect unto you, whosoever of
you are justified by the law; ye
are fallen from grace. For we 5
through the Spirit wait for the
hope of righteousness by faith.
For in Jesus Christ neither circum- 6
cision availeth any thing, nor uncircumcision; but faith which worketh

to being thereby justified. Inasmuch as every such circumcised man places his justification on the ground of legal obedience, he thereby acknowledges his obligation to keep the whole law; and this is the obedience which is not to be expected in the present fallen state of human nature.—The first and last clauses of the 4th verse are equivalent, and express the idea of having no connection with Christ, of having lost the favor of God, or the blessings of a former Gospel condition. Καταργηθῆναι ἀπό, to have become free from, to have nothing more to do with, as in Rom. vii. 2, 6. In the words of Theophylact, "ye who suppose yourselves to be justified by the law, have no fellowship with Christ."* "Are justified:" That is, are aiming to become so, or, in the words just quoted, suppose ye are so. Compare Phil. iii. 9, "my own justification;" that is, such a state of ac- ceptableness with God as attention to the law might be supposed to pro duce. The use of declarative terms which must be modified by the con text, or nature of the case is very common. Thus we have, "delivered, per verting, subverting, seduce," where the intention and endeavor are what is meant. See Gen. xxxvii. 21, Acts xiii. 10, xv. 24, 1 John ii. 26.

5, 6. "Through the Spirit:" The word spirit may denote the spiritual system of the Gospel in contradistinction to the law mentioned in the pre- ceding verse; or it may mean, by the influence of the Holy Spirit, as in ver. 18. The latter seems the more probable view.—" The hope of right- eousness" or justification, is put for the realization of the hope, as the word promise often denotes the thing promised: See Heb. xi. 39, and compare Col. i. 5, Tit. ii. 13, and Heb. vi. 18. Thus it will be equivalent to that future happiness which is the result of justification, and shall be the reward of those who are accepted by God. Ellicott's defence of another view, "We are enabled to cherish the hope of being justified," in accordance with which he translates, "we patiently entertain the hope of righteousness," is not satisfactory. St. Paul would not have presented the Judaizing assump- tion, in contradistinction to the Christian's rightful claim, in such language as this: "Ye think that ye are *already* in possession of justification; we on the contrary *hope for it.*" Neither is it true that "the Christian regarded justifi-

* In loc. Opera, tom. ii. p. 315.

7 by love. Ye did run well; who
   did hinder you, that ye should not
8 obey the truth? This persuasion
   cometh not of him that calleth you.

μένη. Ἐτρέχετε καλῶς· τίς 7
ὑμᾶς ἐνέκοψε τῇ ἀληθείᾳ μὴ
πείθεσθαι; Ἡ πεισμονὴ οὐκ ἐκ 8

---

cation as something *future*," in contrast with "the Jew" who viewed it as
"*present.*" No doubt in its perfection it is future, and, in the words of the quotation from Neander, "stretches into eternity;" and this is also equally true
of redemption and adoption. But it is St. Paul's usage to represent a justified state as that which the true believer has already secured. See, among
other places, Rom. v. 1. Ἀπεκδέχομαι rather expresses *expectation of
something future*, than an *entertaining and cherishing of what is already in
possession*. See Rom. viii. 19, 23, 25, 1 Cor. i. 7, Phil. iii. 20, Heb. ix. 28,
which, with the text under consideration, are the only places in the New
Testament where the word occurs.—The particle γάρ, *for*, is not equivalent
to δέ, *but*. It is illative of the leading thought in the Apostle's mind. It is
as if he had said: 'I implore you not to depend on circumcision or any
external legal ritual, *for* it is only through the Spirit that acceptableness
with God is attainable.'

"In Christ Jesus," &c.: In other words, where the soul is rightly united
to Christ, it is of no importance whether one be circumcised or not; a
living and active faith is everything. Ἐνεργουμένη is middle, and properly expresses the active character of the faith spoken of. It shows itself
working. Observe its use in Rom. vii. 5, 2 Cor. i. 6, iv. 12, Eph. iii. 20.

This verse, so pregnant with meaning, confirms the emphatic signification given to circumcision in ver. 2, and shows also that the faith to which
the Apostle attaches so much importance is not merely the assent of the
understanding, but that principle which bends and forms the character of
the whole inner man, which gives life and practical reality to a Christian
profession. Comp. vi. 15, where a new creature or creation, that is, a moral
and religious condition entirely different from what was before possessed,
and 1 Cor. vii. 19, where holy obedience to God's laws, are contrasted
with circumcision as a merely external rite. The leading idea in these
three parallel places is simply this, that the religion of Christ is internal
and changes the heart.

7. "Persuasion," πεισμονή. This may be understood either actively,
in the sense of application of persuasive arts or skill, or else, passively,
readiness on your part to be persuaded, with the state of mind resulting.
There is an allusion to the preceding verb, πείθεσθαι, to obey, to be persuaded of.—"That called you:" that is, God. See the latter part of the
note on Heb. iii. 1. The Apostle intimates that the persuasion originated
in an opposite source.

9 τοῦ καλοῦντος ὑμᾶς. Μικρὰ
ζύμη ὅλον τὸ φύραμα ζυμοῖ.
10 Ἐγὼ πέποιθα εἰς ὑμᾶς ἐν κυρίῳ,
ὅτι οὐδὲν ἄλλο φρονήσετε· ὁ δὲ
ταράσσων ὑμᾶς βαστάσει τὸ
11 κρίμα, ὅστις ἂν ᾖ. Ἐγὼ δέ,
ἀδελφοί, εἰ περιτομὴν ἔτι κηρύσσω, τί ἔτι διώκομαι ; ἆρα κατήρ-
γηται τὸ σκάνδαλον τοῦ σταυ-

A little leaven leaveneth the whole 9
lump. I have confidence in you 10
through the Lord, that ye will be
none otherwise minded : but he
that troubleth you shall bear his
judgment, whosoever he be. And 11
I, brethren, if I yet preach circumcision, why do I yet suffer persecution? then is the offence of the

9. We have here a caution, in proverbial form, against indulging wrong propensities, and cherishing a state of mind adverse to the Gospel. Some explain the words of erroneous teachers, as if the Apostle had said : ' the allowance of a few to get a footing among you prepares the way for the gradual increase of the number, until they pervade your whole Christian community.' But it seems more in harmony with the context to explain the proverb in relation to any allowance of error, thus : ' What may appear to be a trifling aberration, and confined to no particular point, is likely to extend to most important matters, so as to produce a general state of corruption.' The objection that St. Paul would not characterise the errors referred to as " a little leaven," since he elsewhere speaks of them as grave and serious evils, is not of much weight ; for he may well be supposed to use such language as their advocates would be likely to apply to them. Perhaps both views may be combined. Thus the leaven will be put for the error itself, and also for those influenced by it and active in propagating it.

10. This is probably added to soothe the Galatians, and to assure them that, notwithstanding so great a declension from the simplicity of the Gospel, their spiritual father still cherished a good hope concerning them.—" Ye will be none otherwise minded : " That is, says Borger, ' than what the proverb just employed implies and teaches.' But most probably it is elliptical for, ' that you will harmonize in Christian views, sentiments, and character, with me.' Comp. Phil. ii. 2.—" He that troubleth :" Meaning ' any one who troubles you.' Compare the plural in ver. 12.—" Judgment," sentence : that is, the punishment which follows it.—" Whosoever he be :" This may intimate that some of these erroneous teachers were men of standing and distinction. Or it may be nothing more than a general remark, meaning, ' whatever condition they occupy,' be they rich or poor, learned or unlearned, men of much or little influence.

11. The Apostle here meets the calumny of those who affirmed that he sometimes preached the necessity of circumcision. Such an accusation might plausibly be maintained, as he had circumcised Timothy, and did accommodate occasionally to Jewish rites. See Acts xvi. 3, xviii. 18, xxi.

12 cross ceased. I would they were   ῥοῦ. Ὄφελον καὶ ἀποκόψονται 12
even cut off which trouble you.   οἱ ἀναστατοῦντες ὑμᾶς.

23–26. He repels the charge by saying that, if such were the case, he
would escape persecution, meaning, from the Jews; or else, that the scan-
dal occasioned by the doctrine of Christ crucified had ceased: neither of
which results was true. The first "yet" may refer to his Pharisaic views
before conversion; or it may mean, still, notwithstanding my protestations
to the contrary.

12. "Were cut off:" The verb is in the middle voice. It may be
rendered, 'would cut themselves off,' or 'would for themselves cut off.'
It is doubtful whether the Apostle means to express his wish that these
troublesome perverters of the truth would sever themselves from the
Christian body, or that they would even mutilate and make eunuchs of
themselves, employing a strong and seemingly gross sarcasm. According
to the latter view he will mark their extravagant zeal for external circumcision, by speaking contemptuously, as he does in Phil. iii. 2, 3 : " beware of
the *concision*, for we are the *circumcision*." Chrysostom, Theodoret and
other fathers give this exposition, and so also do some of the ablest of
the modern commentators, among whom are Koppe and Olshausen. It
is maintained also by Robinson, Conybeare and Jowett. The other view,
however, agrees well with the threat, just before announced, that the
troublesome intermeddler shall bear his own punishment, as excision from
the church and its privileges would be. It accords also with 1 Cor. v. 7,
where, after having employed the same proverb as here in ver. 9, he immediately subjoins the direction, " purge out the old leaven;" in other words,
as he directs in ver. 13, " put away from among yourselves that wicked
person."

SECTION V.

Chap. V. 13—VI. 10.

THE CHRISTIAN CONDITION ONE OF SPIRITUAL LIBERTY, AND REQUIRING
CORRESPONDING LIFE AND CONDUCT.   PRACTICAL DIRECTIONS.

13 Ὑμεῖς γὰρ ἐπ᾽ ἐλευθερίᾳ ἐκλήθητε, ἀδελφοί· μόνον μὴ τὴν ἐλευθερίαν εἰς ἀφορμὴν τῇ σαρκί, ἀλλὰ διὰ τῆς ἀγάπης 14 δουλεύετε ἀλλήλοις. Ὁ γὰρ πᾶς νόμος ἐν ἑνὶ λόγῳ πληροῦται, ἐν τῷ· ἀγαπήσεις τὸν πλη- 15 σίον σου ὡς σεαυτόν. Εἰ δὲ ἀλλήλους δάκνετε καὶ κατεσ- θίετε, βλέπετε, μὴ ὑπὸ ἀλλήλων 16 ἀναλωθῆτε. Λέγω δέ, πνεύματι περιπατεῖτε, καὶ ἐπιθυμίαν σαρ-

For, brethren, ye have been called 13 unto liberty; only *use* not liberty for an occasion to the flesh, but by love serve one another. For all 14 the law is fulfilled in one word, *even* in this, Thou shalt love thy neighbour as thyself. But if ye 15 bite and devour one another, take heed that ye be not consumed one of another. *This* I say then, Walk 16 in the Spirit, and ye shall not ful-

13—15. Γάρ· "for: " This is illative. It is as if the Apostle had said, ' You need not be surprised at the earnestness of my language and manner, *for* it is my wish to recall you to the Christian condition of liberty.' The verses contain a suitable caution against such an abuse of Christian liberty as would make it the occasion of sinful indulgence, also an exhortation to mutual love, with a vivid representation of the mischievous consequences of animosity.—The words "liberty" and "serve" are chosen in evident reference to the freedom of Christians from the service of the law, the subject which had been before so fully developed. The sentiment in ver. 14 is to be understood in reference to the context, which limits the application of "law" to that relating to our fellow creatures. See Levit. xix. 18, which is here quoted, and Rom. xiii. 8—10, which contains the same thought. Altercations, contentions, calumnies and evil speaking of each other, bring along with them their appropriate punishment. This is expressed by a figure taken from wild beasts, tearing to pieces and devouring each other.

16. "In" or by "the Spirit:" That is, according to his promptings, as in ver. 18, "if ye be led by the Spirit," and probably in ver. 25. Or, the spirit may be put for the spiritual principle which is implanted by

17 fil the lust of the flesh. For the flesh lusteth against the Spirit, and the Spirit against the flesh: and these are contrary the one to the other; so that ye cannot do 18 the things that ye would. But if ye be led of the Spirit, ye are not 19 under the law. Now the works of the flesh are manifest, which are *these*; Adultery, fornication, 20 uncleanness, lasciviousness, idolatry, witchcraft, hatred, variance, emulations, wrath, strife, seditions, heresies, envyings, murders, 21 drunkenness, revellings, and such like: of the which I tell you before, as I have also told *you* in time past, that they which do such things shall not inherit the kingdom of God. But the fruit of the 22 Spirit is love, joy, peace, long-suffering, gentleness, goodness, faith, 23 meekness, temperance: against such

κὸς οὐ μὴ τελέσητε. Ἡ γὰρ 17 σὰρξ ἐπιθυμεῖ κατὰ τοῦ πνεύματος, τὸ δὲ πνεῦμα κατὰ τῆς σαρκός· ταῦτα δὲ ἀλλήλοις ἀντίκειται, ἵνα μὴ ἃ ἂν θέλητε, ταῦτα ποιῆτε. Εἰ δὲ πνεύματι 18 ἄγεσθε, οὐκ ἐστὲ ὑπὸ νόμον. Φανερὰ δέ ἐστι τὰ ἔργα τῆς σαρ- 19 κός, ἅτινά ἐστι [μοιχεία,] πορ- νεία, ἀκαθαρσία, ἀσέλγεια, εἰδω- 20 λολατρεία, φαρμακεία, ἔχθραι, ἔρεις, ζῆλοι, θυμοί, ἐριθεῖαι, διχοστασίαι, αἱρέσεις, φθόνοι, 21 φόνοι, μέθαι, κῶμοι, καὶ τὰ ὅμοια τούτοις· ἃ προλέγω ὑμῖν, καθὼς καὶ προεῖπον, ὅτι οἱ τὰ τοιαῦτα πράσσοντες βασιλείαν Θεοῦ οὐ κληρονομήσουσιν. Ὁ δὲ καρπὸς 22 τοῦ πνεύματός ἐστιν ἀγάπη, χαρά, εἰρήνη, μακροθυμία, χρησ- τότης, ἀγαθωσύνη, πίστις, πραό- 23 της, ἐγκράτεια· κατὰ τῶν τοιού

the Holy Spirit, and which operates in every Christian mind. This is evidently comprehended in ver. 17, where the spiritual principle and character are antithetic to the carnal, as in Rom. viii. 4–6.—" Fulfil :" better, ' fully do,' as in James ii. 8, 'if ye fully do,' meaning in a sincere and devoted manner.

17. The struggle between the carnal nature and the spiritual principle is here depicted, and as existing even in the regenerate.—"So that ye cannot do the things that ye would :" *Cannot* may convey a true idea, but it is not in the Greek text. If *ἵνα* be telic, the literal translation will be, 'In order that ye may not do those things which ye may wish.' That is, ' the opposition of the flesh to the spirit is intended to produce this result.' This is perfectly true, and the meaning thus obtained is sanctioned by scriptural analogy, as well as by observation and experience. But the words may fairly be rendered, 'so that ye do not those things that ye would.' It is not necessary to regard the particle as telic.

18. If ye are under the guidance of the Spirit or the spiritual principle, then ye are not in subjection to the law, but are in a condition of evangelical liberty. Comp. Rom. vi. 14 : " Sin shall not have dominion over you ; for ye are not under the law, but under grace."

19–23. Now follows a delineation of the fruits respectively of the flesh

24 τῶν οὐκ ἔστι νόμος. Οἱ δὲ τοῦ Χριστοῦ τὴν σάρκα ἐσταύρωσαν σὺν τοῖς παθήμασι καὶ ταῖς 25 ἐπιθυμίαις. Εἰ ζῶμεν πνεύματι, 26 πνεύματι καὶ στοιχῶμεν. Μὴ γινώμεθα κενόδοξοι, ἀλλήλους προκαλούμενοι, ἀλλήλοις φθονοῦντες.

VI. Ἀδελφοί, ἐὰν καὶ προληφθῇ ἄνθρωπος ἔν τινι παραπτώματι, ὑμεῖς οἱ πνευματικοὶ καταρτίζετε τὸν τοιοῦτον ἐν πνεύματι πραότητος· σκοπῶν σεαυτόν, μὴ 2 καὶ σὺ πειρασθῇς. Ἀλλήλων τὰ βάρη βαστάζετε, καὶ οὕτως ἀναπληρώσατε τὸν νόμον τοῦ

there is no law. And they that 24 are Christ's have crucified the flesh with the affections and lusts. If we live in the Spirit, let us also 25 walk in the Spirit. Let us not be 26 desirous of vain glory, provoking one another, envying one another.

Brethren, if a man be overtaken VI. in a fault, ye which are spiritual restore such a one in the spirit of meekness; considering thyself, lest thou also be tempted. Bear ye 2 one another's burdens, and so fulfil

---

and of the spirit, not indeed absolutely perfect, but sufficiently full to show the nature and character of each. The former may be classed under the heads of carnal lusts, superstitious and idolatrous practices, and bitter hatred of others with its natural results. The latter consist of Christian virtues with their happy consequences.—" Of the which I tell you before:" Or, 'forewarn you.' The ἃ is probably governed by κατά understood. With προλέγω compare 1 Thes. iii. 4.—"Fruit of the Spirit:" This figurative word implies the inner influence of the Spirit, showing itself in certain affections and conduct as its natural production. Comp. Matt. iii. 8, Rom. vi. 22, Eph. v. 9.—"Against such there is no law." The Apostle means that such virtues are in perfect unison with the divine law. Comp. 1 Tim. i. 9.

24. "They that are Christ's:" See on iii. 29.

25. "Walk in the Spirit:" That is, pursue the course which he prompts.

26. This verse might well commence a new paragraph. It is closely connected with the next chapter.

vi. 1. "Spiritual:" That is, well instructed and practical Christians, who have attained some standing in the divine life. Comp. 1 Cor. ii. 6, 14, 15, iii. 1, where it is equivalent to "perfect," and contrasted with "carnal" and "natural" or 'animal.'—"Restore:" καταρτίζετε. Literally 'repair.' The word is used for mending and repairing what has been broken. See 1 Cor. i. 10, where it means 'to unite perfectly together,' and occurs in connection with divisions, disunions.

2. Sympathize with and assist each other, as the law of Christ requires.

3 the law of Christ. For if a man think himself to be something, when he is nothing, he deceiveth 4 himself. But let every man prove his own work, and then shall he have rejoicing in himself alone, 5 and not in another: for every man 6 shall bear his own burden. Let him that is taught in the word communicate unto him that teach- 7 eth in all good things. Be not deceived; God is not mocked: for whatsoever a man soweth, that 8 shall he also reap. For he that soweth to his flesh shall of the flesh reap corruption; but he that sow- eth to the Spirit, shall of the Spirit

Χριστοῦ. Εἰ γὰρ δοκεῖ τις εἶναί 3 τι, μηδὲν ὤν, ἑαυτὸν φρεναπατᾷ. Τὸ δὲ ἔργον ἑαυτοῦ δοκιμαζέτω 4 ἕκαστος, καὶ τότε εἰς ἑαυτὸν μόνον τὸ καύχημα ἕξει, καὶ οὐκ εἰς τὸν ἕτερον· ἕκαστος γὰρ τὸ ἴδιον 5 φορτίον βαστάσει. Κοινωνείτω 6 δὲ ὁ κατηχούμενος τὸν λόγον τῷ κατηχοῦντι ἐν πᾶσιν ἀγα- θοῖς. Μὴ πλανᾶσθε· Θεὸς οὐ 7 μυκτηρίζεται· ὃ γὰρ ἐὰν σπείρῃ ἄνθρωπος, τοῦτο καὶ θερίσει· ὅτι ὁ σπείρων εἰς τὴν σάρκα ἑαυτοῦ 8 ἐκ τῆς σαρκὸς θερίσει φθοράν, ὁ δὲ σπείρων εἰς τὸ πνεῦμα ἐκ τοῦ πνεύματος θερίσει ζωὴν

3-5. "Think himself:" The original is simply *seems, appears,* that is, as the context shows, *to himself.*—"Prove;" examine, try.—"And then:" There is an ellipsis to be supplied, thus: 'if such examination be satisfactory.' Comp. 1 Cor. xi. 28: "Let a man examine himself and so," if on examination he is satisfied of his Christian character, "let him eat," &c.—"Rejoicing:" That is, a well founded cause of joy. Olshausen says: "To have rejoicing is to be taken ironically, as ver. 5 shows." But this is quite arbitrary, and the sentiment of ver. 5 naturally arises from the last clause of the preceding verse.—The general meaning of the three verses is as follows: 'If a man over estimates himself, he is self-deceived. Let each one examine his own character and conduct; and then, if he find them to be those of a true Christian, he shall enjoy a satisfaction in his own mind arising from a consciousness of virtue and piety, without any regard to the estimate in which others may hold him. This indeed is of little moment; for as to personal character, and the decision to be formed on it, each indi- vidual must stand for himself.'

6. Let him who is instructed in Christian doctrine impart of his wealth a competency for the support of his instructor.

7, 8. This may be connected with the preceding verse, thus: 'Do not deceive yourselves; you may indeed deride and contemn God's ministers, but he will not allow himself to be thus treated in the person of his servants. If a man devote all his worldly income to the gratification of his own inclina- tions, contributing little or nothing to the support of religion, ruin and misery will be the natural consequence. But if, on the contrary, he is moderate in personal indulgences, and devotes his wealth and efforts to holy and spiritual objects, he shall receive as his appropriate reward everlasting life.' This

9 αἰώνιον. Τὸ δὲ καλὸν ποιοῦντες
  μὴ ἐκκακῶμεν· καιρῷ γὰρ ἰδίῳ
10 θερίσομεν μὴ ἐκλυόμενοι. Ἄρα
  οὖν, ὡς καιρὸν ἔχομεν, ἐργαζώ-
  μεθα τὸ ἀγαθὸν πρὸς πάντας,
  μάλιστα δὲ πρὸς τοὺς οἰκείους
  τῆς πίστεως.

reap life everlasting. And let us 9
not be weary in well doing; for in
due season we shall reap, if we
faint not. As we have therefore 10
opportunity, let us do good unto all
men, especially to them who are
of the household of faith.

---

view agrees well with the context, and most probably with the state of the
Galatians. It is in harmony also with such places as Mark iv. 15, "the
word *sown*," 1 Cor. ix. 11, "if we have *sown* unto you—if we shall *reap*,"
and 2 Cor. ix. 6, 7, "he that *soweth* sparingly shall *reap* also sparingly," &c.
Still it is not necessary to limit the Apostle's application to this particular
point. To sow may be used figuratively for the whole course of preparation made in this life for the future one. The meaning will then be this :
'As are the character and conduct of men now, so shall be their future
condition.' The phraseology is proverbial, as in Job iv. 8, "they that
plough iniquity and sow wickedness, reap the same," and in Prov. xxii. 8,
"he that soweth iniquity shall reap vanity ;" and it occurs in various writings. Koppe and others quote from Aristotle on Rhetoric, Lib. iii. cap. 3,
§ 18, σὺ δὲ ταῦτα αἰσχρῶς μὲν ἔσπειρας, κακῶς δὲ ἐθέρισας· thou hast dis-
gracefully sown, and badly reaped ; and from Cicero de Oratore, Lib. ii.
cap. 65, ut sementem feceris, ita metes.

10. "As we have opportunity :" That is, say some, 'as occasion is afforded us.' But to express this idea accurately, we might expect that the
subjunctive would be used, whereas the original is indicative. Most probably, therefore, the meaning is, 'inasmuch as we have opportunity ;' since
divine Providence has placed us in a condition to be useful.—" The
household of faith :" That is, those who belong to the community of true
Christians. Compare " household of God," in Eph. ii. 19.

SECTION VI.

CHAP. VI. 11–18.

CONCLUSION.

11   Ye see how large a letter I have   ὅΙδετε πηλίκοις ὑμῖν γράμ- 11
written unto you with mine own   μασιν ἔγραψα τῇ ἐμῇ χειρί.

---

11. It has been suggested that the Apostle refers here merely to the concluding verses of the Epistle, and thus marks their importance. But this is wholly unfounded and quite improbable. These verses have no particular importance over the letter in general. His design seems to be to impress the Galatians with the idea of his great regard for them, and his solicitude for their best interests. Therefore, although he generally employed an amanuensis, (see Rom. xvi. 22, 1 Cor. xvi. 21, 2 Thess. iii. 17,) he here states that he wrote to them with his own hand, in order to make the deeper impression. It is uncertain whether πηλίκοις γράμμασι translated, "how large a letter," refers to the length of the Epistle, or the size and shape of the letters. The latter construction would be, 'with what large letters.' According to this view, which is maintained by Chrysostom, Theodoret, Theophylact and Jerome,* in loc., among the ancients, and also by some modern critics, St. Paul may allude to some difficulty which he had in writing. This has been supposed to be connected with the weakness referred to in iv. 13, 14, which may have affected his nervous system. But, in this case he would probably have stated the difficulty, and told the Galatians plainly of the effort he had been obliged to make in order to show his anxiety to advance their spiritual interests. It has also been suggested that a person accustomed to write in Hebrew would naturally form his Greek letters bulky and stiff. This, however, would depend upon the structure of the Hebrew written character of that period. Besides, the largeness of letters does not warrant the supposition of any stiffness or want of elegance in the shape.—The words may be translated, 'in what letters,' meaning 'how many,' and be used here in the sense of copiously, largely. Neander thinks it best to allow a slight inaccuracy in the use of πηλίκοις for πόσοις, as, in the later Latin, quanti, how great, is often

---

* Jerome refers the phrase to the Apostle's chirography, which, he thinks, was known to the Galatians, and which extended from this verse to the end of the Epistle, and showed itself in the different formation of the letters from those of the preceding portion. Opera, Tom. iv. Col. 314, 315.

12 Ὅσοι θέλουσιν εὐπροσωπῆσαι ἐν σαρκί, οὗτοι ἀναγκάζουσιν ὑμᾶς περιτέμνεσθαι, μόνον ἵνα τῷ σταυρῷ τοῦ Χριστοῦ μὴ διώκων·

hand. As many as desire to make 12 a fair shew in the flesh, they constrain you to be circumcised; only lest they should suffer persecution

---

employed for quot, how many.*—The plural may be used for a single letter, like litera in Latin. If the phrase refers, as most probably it does, to the length of the letter, it must be regarded as comparative, the nature of the subject being considered, for it is shorter than those to the Romans and Corinthians, and not longer than that to the Ephesians. The word commonly employed by St. Paul to denote a letter is ἐπιστολή as in 1 Cor. v. 9, 2 Cor. x. 10, and elsewhere. St. Luke uses γράμματα in Acts xxviii. 21, where, however, it is probable that more than one letter is intended. And so also in 1 Macc. v. 10, where the Israelites are said to have "sent letters, γράμματα, to Judas and his brethren," which are referred to in ver. 14 as αἱ ἐπιστολαί. In Ignatius to the Romans, sect. 8, to which Ellicott refers, δι' ὀλίγων γραμμάτων most probably means the letters which compose the Epistle. In 2 Kings xix. 14 we have הַסְּפָרִים, rendered in our translation "the letter," followed by a plural and then a singular suffix, and in the Septuagint βιβλία with plural pronouns twice; yet there was but one letter. In the parallel place, Isa. xxxvii. 14, both the suffixes are singular, and the Septuagint has βιβλίον, followed twice by singular pronouns. It is difficult to determine whether the true meaning is, 'in how large a letter,' or, 'in what large letters.'

12. " To make a fair show in the flesh :" That is, to exhibit a specious exterior in outward observances. "Lest they should suffer persecution for the cross of Christ," τῷ σταυρῷ τοῦ Χριστοῦ. Conybeare translates: " to save themselves from the persecution which Christ bore upon the cross;" adding in a note, "literally, persecution inflicted by the cross of Christ." The idea conveyed by the translation is, 'such persecution as Christ sustained on the cross;' whereas that expressed in the note is, 'persecution occasioned by the cross.' Jowett says: "These words may be translated,—'only that they may not be persecuted by the cross of Christ,'— that is, may not have fellowship with the sufferings of Christ." It is not easy to perceive how *being persecuted by the cross* can be equivalent to *having fellowship with the sufferings*. He does not defend this interpretation, but thinks " it better to take the words according to a less common usage of the dative, found also in classical Greek, in the sense, 'because of the cross of Christ,' " as no doubt it is. " The dative points out the *ground* or *cause* of the persecution : Rom. xi. 20, *were broken off* τῇ ἀπιστίᾳ, *on account of unbelief.*" Ellicott. The danger of persecution from Jews

---

* Geschichte der Pflanzung, &c., p. 194, note 1.

13 for the cross of Christ. For neither they themselves who are circumcised keep the law; but desire
to have you circumcised, that they
14 may glory in your flesh. But God
forbid that I should glory, save in
the cross of our Lord Jesus Christ,
by whom the world is crucified
unto me, and I unto the world.
15 For in Christ Jesus neither circumcision availeth any thing, nor uncircumcision, but a new creature.

ται. Οὐδὲ γὰρ οἱ περιτεμνόμενοι 13
αὐτοὶ νόμον φυλάσσουσιν, ἀλλὰ
θέλουσιν ὑμᾶς περιτέμνεσθαι,
ἵνα ἐν τῇ ὑμετέρᾳ σαρκὶ καυχή-
σωνται. Ἐμοὶ δὲ μὴ γένοιτο 14
καυχᾶσθαι εἰ μὴ ἐν τῷ σταυρῷ
τοῦ κυρίου ἡμῶν Ἰησοῦ Χριστοῦ,
δι' οὗ ἐμοὶ κόσμος ἐσταύρωται
κἀγὼ τῷ κόσμῳ. Ἐν γὰρ Χρισ- 15
τῷ Ἰησοῦ οὔτε περιτομή τι ἔστιν
οὔτε ἀκροβυστία, ἀλλὰ καινὴ

would be the more easily avoided on the part of the Galatians, by acceding
to the " desire " of the Judaizers.—Perhaps the Apostle may refer also to
annoyances and private persecutions by which the more rigid adherents of
the law might be able to distress converts who acted in the manner here
advocated by St. Paul. Compare ii. 12, v. 11, and see also Acts xxi. 27, 28.

13, 14. The statements in the first of these verses were applicable both
to the unconverted Jews, and to the party in the Christian church which
affected extraordinary devotion to the law. Neither of them made efforts
to keep its moral precepts, but insisted on the observance of circumcision
and other external rites, in order to boast of the number and devotion of
their adherents. But, on the other hand, the object of the Apostle's glory-
ing is none other than the system of Christ crucified as an atonement for
sin, thus abolishing the ritual law, (see Eph. ii. 15, Col. ii. 14,) laying a
solid foundation for acceptance with God, and destroying all connection
between the world and the believer. Comp. ver. 12, and 1 Cor. i. 18, latter half.

15. " In Christ Jesus:" " That is," says Olshausen, " in his body, the
church." But this is not the meaning of the phrase, which always denotes
the true Christian's union with Christ. To be in the church regarded as his
mystical body does indeed imply such a union, but the words directly express the believer's spiritual connection with his Redeemer and head.
It may here be paraphrased thus : 'In reference to union with Christ Jesus.' For the general sentiment of the verse, see on v. 6.

" New creature" or creation : This implies a thorough change of condition and character, both in reference to external covenant relations to
God, and also to the internal divine life. The complete establishment of
Messiah's Kingdom is represented by the prophets under the figure of a
new creation. Thus Isaiah : " Behold I create new heavens and a new
earth ; I create Jerusalem a rejoicing and her people a joy. The new heavens and the new earth which I will make shall remain before me, saith

16 κτίσις. Καὶ ὅσοι τῷ κανόνι
τούτῳ στοιχήσουσιν, εἰρήνη ἐπ'
αὐτοὺς καὶ ἔλεος, καὶ ἐπὶ τὸν
17 Ἰσραὴλ τοῦ Θεοῦ. Τοῦ λοιποῦ
κόπους μοι μηδεὶς παρεχέτω·
ἐγὼ γὰρ τὰ στίγματα τοῦ κυρίου
Ἰησοῦ ἐν τῷ σώματί μου βασ-

And as many as walk according to 16
this rule, peace be on them, and
mercy, and upon the Israel of God.
From henceforth let no man trouble 17
me; for I bear in my body the

---

the Lord :" lxv. 17, 18, lxvi. 22.   Comp. 2 Pet. iii. 13, Rev. xxi. 1.   This
new creation takes place partly in the present state in the regeneration of
men by the agency of the Spirit, thus bringing them in the church of God
within the sphere of his holy influences, and completely in the future by
the resurrection of the regenerate in spiritual and incorruptible bodies, and
their admission into the kingdom of glory.   Restoration to a primitive
state of holy innocence is represented as a new creation, although it is properly a re-formation of the whole inner man.   Hence David prays : " Create in me a clean heart, O God, and renew a right spirit within me :" Ps.
li. 10.   Such language is of very frequent occurrence in the epistles.   Thus
in Eph. ii. 10 : " We are his workmanship, created in Christ Jesus."   We
read also : " God hath wrought us ;" and, " if any man be in Christ, he is a
new creature," and, " the new man is created according to God in righteousness and true holiness :" 2 Cor. v. 5, 17, Eph. iv. 24.   With the last passage compare Col. iii. 10, where the word is " renewed."   Hence the divine
omnipotence which effected the resurrection of Christ is represented as the
source of the spiritual blessings which God imparts to the believer, comprehending his present moral and future glorious resurrection and elevation ; (see Eph. i. 19, 20, Col. ii. 12 :) and he who, at the creation of the
chaotic mass, called light into existence, is said to have " shined into our
hearts :" 2 Cor. iv. 6.   All this implies a different state of being and
character from a former one.

16. " This rule :" Meaning that implied in the sentiment of the preceding verse.   The verb be is not in the text, and the ellipsis might as well
be supplied with shall be.   " The Israel of God :" This phraseology may
be equivalent to Abraham's spiritual descendants, that is, true Christians,
whether of Jewish or Gentile extraction : See iii. 29.   In this case, the καί
will be exegetical, as it sometimes is.   Still it is not improbable that St.
Paul may have intended a special reference to his converted countrymen,
to whom his mind habitually turned, and towards whom his heart ever
warmed.

17. Τοῦ λοιποῦ· χρόνου is most probably to be supplied, and the
meaning, as given in our authorised version, "from henceforth," hereafter.   It may be equivalent to the author's ordinary conclusions ; but his

18 marks of the Lord Jesus. Breth-
ren, the grace of our Lord Jesus
Christ *be* with your spirit: Amen.
Unto the Galatians, written from
Rome.

τάζω. Ἡ χάρις τοῦ κυρίου 18
ἡμῶν Ἰησοῦ Χριστοῦ μετὰ τοῦ
πνεύματος ὑμῶν, ἀδελφοί· ἀμήν.
Πρὸς Γαλάτας ἐγράφη ἀπὸ
Ῥώμης

---

usual word is λοιπόν with or without the article: See 2 Cor. xiii. 11,
Eph. vi. 10, Phil. iv. 8. The genitive form never elsewhere occurs in the
New Testament.

"The marks of the Lord Jesus:" That is, the wounds, and external
signs of persecution endured for Christ's sake, which marked the Apostle
as his servant. See 2 Cor. i. 5, iv. 10, xi. 23, 24. The phraseology seems
to have been chosen in reference to the practice of branding slaves, or
marking persons who consecrated themselves to the service of some particular deity. See the passages from ancient writers cited by Borger, and
other commentators in loc. Thus the Apostle will intimate that the marks
of his varied persecutions were proof of his belonging to Christ, and therefore ought to be regarded as satisfactory evidence of his sincerity and devotion, and relieve him from any further annoyance.

QUESTIONS ON THE PRECEDING EXPOSITION.

The reader is requested to observe that the page is noted immediately after the questions founded on it.

INTRODUCTION.

WHO were the Galatians?—By whom were they converted to Christianity? p. ix.—Is there any doubt respecting the time and occasion of this event?—What is the most probable result of the inquiry? ix. x.—At what time and place is it most probable that the Epistle was written? xi.–xii.—Of whom did the Galatian churches consist?—What was the nature of the error into which they had fallen?—Is it possible to determine of what particular class the party opposed to St. Paul consisted?—In what respects does he vindicate himself, and what authority does he claim?—What error in reference to justification does he refute?—In what respect does the Epistle coincide with that to the Romans? xii. xiii.

SECTION I.—CHAP. III.

WHAT does St. Paul begin by declaring? 1.—How does he defend his claim to a direct divine commission?—State the two leading views of the first verses of Acts xiii: 11, 12.—Who are meant by "the brethren" whom he associates with himself in writing? 12.—What is implied in the language, "gave himself for our sins?" 13.—At what does the Apostle express his surprise and astonishment? 1, 13.—Who is meant by "him that called you?" 14.—Explain the connection of vs. 6, 7: 15.—What was the occasion of the perversion of the Galatians: 1, 15.—From what charge does the author vindicate himself?—And how? 2, 16.—State what particulars he here gives of his former life: 2, 3, 16 et seq.—Did he derive all his knowledge of the facts and truths of Christianity directly from divine revelation? 16.—Explain the phrases, "separated me from my mother's womb—revealed his Son in me—flesh and blood:" 17.—Why did he go to Arabia? 18, 19.—From what point are the three years mentioned in ver. 18 to be reckoned? 19.—How many Apostles were named James? 20.—Is this visit to Jerusalem probably mentioned elsewhere? 21.—How does the remark of ver. 22 bear upon the leading topic in the Apostle's mind? 22.—Of which visit to Jerusalem does St. Paul here speak?—Mention his other visits to that city.—From what period are the fourteen years to be computed? 22.—Show the consistency of his appointment as a delegate with his going in consequence of a revelation:—

Why did he make a private statement to the prominent men ? 23.—Give the leading views of vs. 3–5 : 23–26.—Does the translation "committed unto me" in ver. 7 accord with New Testament usage ?—Explain the words "circumcision—uncircumcision—grace—pillars:" 27.—What "poor" are here referred to ?—What is the true meaning of the word translated "to be blamed ?" 28.—On what account did the Apostle censure St. Peter? 28, 29.—Had he any particular motive for calling attention to this censure ?—Mention an ancient unfounded conjecture, and equally unfounded opinion : 30.—State the different views of the extent of the address to St. Peter : 30.—Also, its general tenor : 31, 32.—Can the time of this interview between the two Apostles be positively settled ?—State the principal views on this point : 32, 33.—How does St. Paul defend his own consistency ? 3, 4, 33.—Explain the 18th verse : 33.—Also, the meaning of, " I through the law am dead to the law :" 34.—Are verses 20, 21 a continuance of the figure begun in ver. 19, or is there a transition to a different sort of deadness ? 34, 35.

Section II.—Chap. III.

What are the general points comprehended within this section ? 4, 35.—What is implied in the phrase " bewitched you ?"—What does the figure in the latter part of the first verse denote ?—How does the writer show the absurd procedure of the Galatians ?—How is the word " faith" here used ? 35, 36.—What is the force of the words " spirit" and " flesh" when contrasted ?—Show the meaning of the phrases, " yet in vain ;" and, " who are of faith:" 37.—Explain and vindicate the Apostle's declaration that " the Scripture preached the Gospel to Abraham :" 38, 39.—What is denoted by the preposition " with" in ver. 9 ?—Is the phrase, " of the works of the law," to be limited to the idea of mere connection ?—State the logical force of the particle " for:" 39.—Explain the quotations in vs. 10, 12, and show how the Apostle employs them : 40; also, that in ver. 11.—What idea is conveyed by the word, " redeemed?" 41 ; by the phrase, " the promise of the Spirit ?" 41, 42.—What does the Apostle proceed to show in ver. 15 and seq. 4, 5, 42.—What is meant by the phrase, " speak after the manner of men ?"—What proposition does he lay down as the foundation of his argument ?—Prove that he has a *covenant* and not a *testament* in view: 42, 43.—Does he here argue from the singular word " seed ?"—State some of the views and embarrassments which have sprung from this supposition : 44, 45.—Give his meaning, on the supposition that he is not arguing but merely interpreting: 45, 46.—Explain the full import of the words, " thy seed, which is Christ:" 46.—Does the force of the Apostle's argument depend upon the length of the period ? 47.—State the two general views respecting the time of the Israelites' residence in

Egypt, with the arguments in support of each: 47–49.—Did St. Paul regard the inheritance promised to Abraham as limited to the possession of Palestine? 49.—What reason is here given for the subsequent addition of the law? 49.—Explain the meaning of "ordained by angels:" 50.—Give some of the leading views of ver. 20: 51–56.—In illustrating the truth that God's law and promise are not contradictory, what does the Apostle say of the former?—Explain the words, "the Scripture hath shut up all under sin:"—the meaning of "faith" in this connection, and "schoolmaster:" 57, 58.—Show the force of "for" in vs. 26, 27.—What is the import of "baptized into, put on, Christ?" 59.—What is the idea conveyed in ver. 28? 60.

SECTION III.—CHAP. IV. 1–20.

WHAT two conditions are illustrated in this section? and what image is employed? 6, 60, 61.—Explain the phrases, "elements of the world—fulness of the time:" 61.—State the general thought in ver. 6: 62.—Explain the difference of phraseology here and in Rom. viii. 15.—What is the meaning of the words, "Spirit of his Son?" 63.—How does the Apostle show the Galatians their inconsistency in relapsing into an external system? 63, 64.—Explain the words, "are known of God:" 64.—Give the two leading views of ver. 12: 65, 66.—What is intended by the clauses, "through infirmity of the flesh—my temptation in the flesh?" 66–69.—Explain the terms, "as an angel of God—blessedness—plucked out your eyes:" 69.—Give the general meaning of vs. 17, 18: 70.—"My little children:" Is this the best translation?—Show the force of the Apostle's figure: 71.

SECTION IV.—CHAP. IV. 21—V. 12.

STATE the general contents of this section: 8, 9, 72.—How is the word "law" here employed? 72.—"An allegory:" Give the true translation.—State the two views of which the words are susceptible, and defend the true one: 73–76.—Does St. Paul argue from the meaning of the word Hagar? 76.—What is meant by "the above Jerusalem?" 77.—Explain the meaning and application of Isa. liv. 1.—Explain also, "children of promise—after the Spirit:" 78.—How is it that Ishmael is said to have "persecuted" Isaac? 79.—What application of the language of Gen. xxi. 10 is intended in ver. 30? 79.—Why does St. Paul introduce his own name in v. 2?—Explain the words, "if ye be circumcised—are justified:" 80, 81.—What is meant by waiting for the hope of justification? 81, 82.—What is the sentiment of ver. 6? 82.—Explain the proverbial expression in ver. 9: 83.—What is meant by, "were cut off?" 84.

7

Section V.—Chap. V. 13—VI. 10.

State the leading points of this section : 9.—What is the force of the particle "for ?"—What caution is here contained, and how is the exhortation drawn out ? 85.—What is depicted in ver. 17, and the true translation of the latter clause ? 86.—What is implied in the phrase, "fruit of the Spirit ?"—Explain the epithet "spiritual" in vi. 1 : 87.—What is the general meaning of vs. 3–5 ? 88.—State the meaning and connection of vs. 7, 8 : 88, 89.—What is implied in the expression, " as we have opportunity ?" 89.

Section VI.—Chap. VI. 11–18.

" How large a letter ?" State the principal views which have been taken of this phrase : 90, 91.—Explain the words, "in Christ Jesus—new creature" or creation—" Israel of God :" 92, 93.—What does the Apostle mean by " marks of the Lord Jesus ?" 94.

THE END.

www.ingramcontent.com/pod-product-compliance
Lightning Source LLC
Chambersburg PA
CBHW071145090426
42736CB00012B/2227